SAIS
PAPERS IN INTERNATIONAL AFFAIRS

The Challenge to U.S. Policy in the Third World

Global Responsibilities and Regional Devolution

Thomas Perry Thornton

WESTVIEW PRESS/BOULDER AND LONDON
SCHOOL OF ADVANCED INTERNATIONAL STUDIES
THE JOHNS HOPKINS UNIVERSITY

NUMBER 10

SAIS
PAPERS IN INTERNATIONAL AFFAIRS

The Challenge to U.S. Policy in the Third World

Global Responsibilities and Regional Devolution

Thomas Perry Thornton

WESTVIEW PRESS/BOULDER AND LONDON
WITH THE FOREIGN POLICY INSTITUTE
SCHOOL OF ADVANCED INTERNATIONAL STUDIES
THE JOHNS HOPKINS UNIVERSITY

A Westview Press / Foreign Policy Institute Edition

Published in 1986 in the United States of America by Westview Press, Inc.; Frederick A. Praeger, Publisher; 5500 Central Avenue, Boulder, Colorado 80301

Library of Congress Cataloging-in-Publication Data
Thornton, Thomas Perry.
  The challenge to U.S. policy in the Third World.
  (SAIS papers in international affairs; no. 10)
  Includes index.
  1. Developing countries—Foreign relations—United
States. 2. United States—Foreign relations—Developing
countries. 3. United States—Foreign relations—
1945– . I. Title. II. Title: Challenge to US
policy in the Third World. III. Series.
D888.U6T46 1986   327.730172′4   86-11097
ISBN 0-8133-7076-0

Printed and bound in the United States of America

The paper used in this publication meets the requirements of the American National Standard for Permanence of Paper for Printed Library Materials Z39.48-1984.

10   9   8   7   6   5   4   3   2   1

ABOUT THE BOOK AND AUTHOR

In formulating policy toward the Third World, U.S. decisionmakers have been hampered by a superficial understanding of events in developing countries, by a tendency to deal with Third World problems in terms of global considerations, and by the role of the United States as a superpower with responsibility for helping to manage regional security affairs. In the past decade, however, a number of Third World states have become increasingly able to handle their own security requirements. Thomas Thornton argues that it is imperative for the United States to play a role in this process of devolution of security responsibility if the United States is to protect its own national security interests and maintain the global military-strategic balance. His review of five areas—South Asia, Southeast Asia, the Gulf, Southern Africa, and Central America—shows that there are various degrees of promise for resolution of regional problems by regional powers. Mr. Thornton points out that to assist in the development of regional responsibility, U.S. policy must balance the importance of global and regional considerations with a recognition of the capabilities of Third World countries themselves.

Thomas Perry Thornton is adjunct professor of Soviet and Asian studies at The Johns Hopkins School of Advanced International Studies. During the Carter administration he was in charge of North-South affairs on the staff of the National Security Council.

To Karin
and to
Tommy, Nalini, and Peter

CONTENTS

INTRODUCTION

$\mathbf{M}$Y PURPOSE IN THIS book is to demonstrate that there are some overall strategies that can be applied when determining U.S. policy toward the countries of the Third World. To be useful, this type of book must be directed to a diversity of readers—all those who are concerned with the subject, whether policymakers, academic analysts, or members of the general public.

The subject matter and audience require a presentation with an extremely broad scope, embracing both globalist and regionalist strains of the ongoing policy debate. It has to deal with policy across the full range of countries in the Third World. This means passing over a lot of detail on the assumption that the reader is generally familiar with the subject matter. It also entails considerable generalization about an entity—the Third World—that is amorphous at best. Finally, only a few parts of the Third World can be examined in detail, and these not always in equal depth. The choice of audience dictates the manner of presentation. A work that is mainly analytical and presented in traditional scholarly form would not be read by the policymakers, who need it most, whereas one without an articulated theoretical underpinning would probably be of little use in providing the kind of constructive approach that I will be suggesting.

I make these points as an apologia rather than an apology, for effective policy presentation, no less than policymaking, must stay on the middle ground if it is to achieve the necessary broad base of understanding and support. This country's policy toward the Third World has unfortunately not received much understanding or support over any sustained period.

In Chapter 1 I specifically address this problem—the changes in American attitudes toward the Third World during the past several decades; my concern in Chapter 2 is the international environment in which our policy toward the Third World is conducted. Dramatic shifts have occurred in the power structure of this environment: Not only has the power of the Soviet Union greatly increased, but, equally important for our concerns, the power and capability within the Third World itself have also grown. In Chapter 3 I examine the implications of these changes and set forth a conceptual framework to help the reader understand the direction of change and put it in perspective.

Chapters 4 and 5 deal with U.S. interests and policy choices regarding the Third World. Interests are no more immutable than are capabilities, and it is useful to attempt a net assessment, even if sketchy, of the interrelated sets of changes in our interests, attitudes, and capabilities, and in the capabilities of others. Several policy choices emerge from this calculation: The one I find most useful lies in the familiar middle ground—a policy of purposeful devolution of responsibility for security maintenance from the superpowers to individual states and especially to groupings of states in several regions of the Third World. Although this policy certainly is not novel, it has become much more interesting in light of the changes that have taken place in the international environment and within the Third World itself.

In Chapter 6 I examine five such regional groupings in different parts of the Third World. My choice reflects both the illustrative value of the individual cases and a necessary geographic spread. Although the results are predictably mixed, they provide striking evidence of an emerging pattern compatible with the specific areas addressed, consistent with the kind of world described in the opening chapters and not inconsistent with different approaches that will have to be taken in parts of the world where conditions make a policy of devolution unconvincing.

Finally in Chapter 7, I attempt to pull together these various strands to articulate more specifically what a concept of devolution does (and does not) entail, to consider the problems of bringing the policy establishment to address the Third World in these terms, and to suggest how such a policy can most effectively be pursued. In particular, I return to the five regions of the Third World examined in Chapter 6, this time asking what requirements would be needed for a conscious design of evolution that differ from what has been and is now being done.

Most recent U.S. administrations have committed themselves to and often pursued policies consistent with devolution of security responsibility to those most directly concerned. What has been lacking—often dangerously so—is a conceptual framework within which ad hoc policies can be related to an overall goal and pursued in those terms. That is why I found this book worth writing and, I trust, worth reading: Until we come to terms with such a concept, the prospects for long-term stability and success in U.S. Third World policy are uncertain at best.

Several terms need to be defined before I begin my discussion. The outlines of the various regions in the Third World are extremely fluid. Although in several case studies, I have made some attempts at definition, most regions have fuzzy boundaries in reality. The word *regionalism* connotes something more than the activities of groups of neighboring states: It implies a concern with both regions and individual Third World countries, as opposed to concern with the superpower rivalry or other manifestations of the global system. Because it would be tedious to repeatedly write "regions and individual countries," I shall use the term *regions* to cover both. The term *security management* is used to describe the political and military activity of one or more states to ensure that they, or a region in which they are located, are not rent with conflict, do not become a burden on the international order, and do not develop into a battleground in the cold war because of their own internal divisions. I use the term *access* to cover a vast range of activities that one nation may want to pursue with regard to another. At the upper end it can involve domination or military alliances; at the lower end it may mean little more than a routine level of international contact that would characterize the relations of, say, Canada and the Ivory Coast.

Although a wealth of literature is devoted to describing some part of the Third World, not many studies usefully discuss the various parts in a global context. There is good reason for this: It is nearly impossible for one author to cover such a broad range of material adequately and parceling out assignments to several authors with regional specialties is rarely satisfactory. Because it seems worthwhile to put a larger picture together, I will attempt to do so, recognizing that the product cannot be fully satisfactory in detail. Most of the literature that does approach the Third World in broad terms is concerned primarily with economic matters—and understandably so, given the needs of those countries. This study, however, is almost exclusively concerned with security and political matters, subjects that occupy much of the "higher" policy dialogue between the United States and the Third World and that are the most important determinants of U.S. policy. To the extent that the economic dialogue does not simply follow a path of its own (e.g., much of the North-South debate), it can, in its specifics, be adapted readily to the kind of approach suggested here.

In an undertaking of this sort, an author owes it to the readers to explain himself. My background is primarily in the federal government, where I have had the opportunity to address the subject matter of this study at a variety of levels. My area specialty is South Asia (the Indo-

Pakistan subcontinent), with which I have dealt for a large part of my working life. During the Nixon and Ford administrations I served as senior member of the Department of State Policy Planning Staff and was responsible not only for South Asia but also for global issues and U.S.-Soviet relations. For the four years of the Carter administration, I was head of North-South affairs on the National Security Council Staff where, aside from the broader duties implied in that title, I became more deeply involved in African and Latin American affairs.

Besides my experience in the federal government, I have had several opportunities to work in an academic setting. Since 1982, I have been associated with the School of Advanced International Studies (SAIS) of Johns Hopkins University, on a dual appointment as adjunct professor in the Department of Asian Studies and as an associate of the Johns Hopkins Foreign Policy Institute. SAIS has generously provided me with a home for these four years and with facilities to pursue my interests. The Foreign Policy Institute kindly organized a series of meetings to discuss the topics covered in this book and has undertaken its publication. My gratitude goes to the participants at those meetings, especially Evelyn Colbert, Richard Feinberg, Ambassadors Stephen Low and James Spain, and my SAIS colleagues Robert Lystad, Nathaniel Thayer, and I. William Zartman. I owe a particular debt to three cherished friends and sometime colleagues who took time to make detailed, helpful comments on an earlier draft—William Barnds, Paul Kreisberg, and Howard Wriggins. Piero Gleijeses, Wolf Grabendorff, and Martin Lowenkopf provided helpful comments on specific sections. None of the individuals or organizations named is, of course, responsible for what I have written, and neither the Department of State nor the National Security Council staff is necessarily associated with any of my views.

To write a study with a broad scope, the author draws on a vast array of sources, whether books or personal contacts. The opportunities for citations are infinite, but I have held them to an absolute minimum. To indicate some of my more important intellectual debts and offer suggestions for further readings, I have provided brief bibliographic notes for the individual chapters. There is no way to express my gratitude and indebtedness to my colleagues in the American foreign-policy establishment, who have been my guides over the past decades. I thank them all—collectively, anonymously, and profusely.

1.
THE TWILIGHT OF AMERICAN EXCEPTIONALISM

A Perplexing World

For many Americans who came of age in the years following World War II, the world has become a perplexing and disappointing place. Those of us who grew up in the heady years of undisputed U.S. primacy have seen power seemingly slip from our country's hands, and we cannot understand just how or why it has happened. The United States still exerts immense economic, political, and military power, but the younger generation (in particular) now questions the morality, usability, and righteousness of this seemingly flawed power. No one can contemplate this country's using its vast and costly nuclear arsenal, and since Vietnam few causes have surfaced for which Americans would be willing to die. Even our economic power has been undermined, not just by external competition like Japanese imports, but also by the 1982 debt crisis in several developing countries—an experience that taught us that our own economic strength could be held hostage against us.

If U.S. power were merely flawed, a refocusing of national will could bring it to bear and restore our previous leadership. Our power is, however, much more limited than before: While our capabilities have grown in absolute terms, those of other countries have been increasing at a much more rapid rate. The U.S. writ simply does not run as far as it did in the past. Furthermore, in security terms, the United States is facing the dilemma that has confronted nations throughout history: insufficient strength to independently protect all vital interests against all likely threats. In the starkest terms, U.S. nuclear strategy accepts the fact that millions of Americans would die in a general war, a position that virtually abandons the most vital interest we have. In other vital areas as well, we find we cannot unilaterally ensure that our country will have an adequate supply of oil, and we can no longer impose our will on nearby countries that formerly enjoyed sovereignty at our tolerance.

The challenge of the international system lies not only in the more traditional differences and interaction between political (security) and economic aspects, but also in the rise of a new set of global issues, which transcend and impact politics and economics. As the nations of the world have become more self-aware and interdependent, human rights, ocean mining, climate modification, degradation of the ecology, nuclear proliferation, and other issues have appeared on the international agenda without universally accepted methods for dealing with them. Yet they must be dealt with on a global basis because their impact is global. Global unity is, however, still an ideal because the structure of our world is complex and fluid, and it is defined by conflict as well as by cooperation.

The East-West division in the international system, which became institutionalized after World War II, continues, and it is further widened by an even more pervasive fault line reflecting North-South differences. The problems caused by a host of new nations in the Third World present a greater challenge to the United States than the more traditional kinds of problems presented by Europe and Japan, which have come to rival us in productivity, affluence, and social justice, or by the Soviet Union, which has achieved parity in some of the most critical aspects of military strength. In the Third World the gap between absolute power and usable power is most striking. For instance, many of these countries cannot even remotely match the United States in military or economic strength, and yet we are often unable to exert any real influence over their thoughts or actions on matters of importance to us. Also in the Third World the possibility of Soviet gains is most threatening because the governments of these countries are frequently unstable and they are not anchored in NATO-like defense treaties or irrevocably tied to the West by culture, tradition, or politics. Finally, Americans believe that they have poured vast sums of money and national effort into the Third World with frequently disappointing results. With few exceptions— mostly in East Asia—our efforts have been at best unappreciated; at worst they have seemed wasted.

Americans find it difficult to understand that the newly independent countries of the Third World view the international scene in very different ways than we do. If the American experience has universal relevance, why do many countries look for other paths and consciously reject the United States as their natural ally? We (and incidentally, the Soviets no less) assumed that the interests of the developing countries largely coincided with our own, especially in security terms and also in politics and economics. When we look beyond the speeches made by visiting leaders of developing countries, we find that in country after country, the United States is seen not as a natural ally or a benevolent protector but as a source of concern.

Third World countries view the United States with unease not simply because we could touch off a nuclear war but also because our very size and strength seem threatening. Mexico does not need ominous threats from Washington to worry about its U.S. neighbor. Just as France will always be uneasy next to Germany, Pakistan to India, and Greece to Turkey, Mexicans will see us as a potential threat, no matter how soothing our rhetoric or even how wise our policies. Mexico is, of course, the extreme case since it is a neighbor, but most Latin American countries share the Mexicans' feelings, as do more distant countries whose economies depend on ours. Other countries have a more tangible reason for seeing the United States as a potential threat: Gulf Arabs regard the United States not only as the patron of their principal enemy, Israel, but also as the only country that has talked about using force to ensure the flow of oil. Although Indians should have a much more lively fear of the Soviet Union because of its proximity and its invasion of Afghanistan, they recall that the United States—not the Soviet Union— threatened them with armed force during their 1971 war with Pakistan.

Recognition of the potential threat that the United States poses does not necessarily entail criticism of U.S. actions or statements, much less acceptance of arguments that the United States is inherently dangerous, interventionist, or evil. Despite profound concerns about the size and power of the United States, most Third World countries find it handy to have us around: In a threatening international atmosphere, the United States is a useful stabilizer, source of military support, economic donor, cornucopia of technology, and place to send children to school or perhaps to get a green card. Even so, though most Third World countries have come to regard the United States as a more welcome international neighbor than the Soviet Union, not many see a qualitative difference between this country and the Soviet Union. The United States is just another superpower, respected but mistrusted.

The United States cannot pay, coerce, or cajole most Third World countries into supporting its unilaterally proclaimed causes. Though the hope of restoring past influence appeals to some Americans, the cost would be enormous and the outcome uncertain; bitterness and a resort to our tradition of isolationism are ready but inadequate answers. Even less can be said for resorting to an orgy of self-recrimination for the misperceived sins of the past—another American tradition. The entire relationship between the United States and the Third World is ambiguous. Third World nations' doubts about the United States are mirrored in this country's doubts about them. Still we must do business with each other, and this relationship requires us to learn to live with complex and partial answers.

This study attempts to better define some of the problems inherent in U.S.–Third World relations and to suggest some partial solutions. It presents perspectives on the United States, its historical experience in dealing with the Third World, and the traumatic changes that this country has gone through. The central problem is, of course, that the international environment is in the midst of a vast reordering. In an incredibly short time the whole imperial structure has been refashioned, and power has passed, on one hand, to the two hostile superpowers and, on the other, from the European metropoles to Asia, Africa, and Latin America. Barely able to cope with the first of these changes, the United States needs to effectively come to terms with the second, while maintaining a balance between the two. This dilemma is the traditional one between globalism and regionalism, and it provides part of the framework for my analysis.

In this study my focus is not the maintenance of the U.S. strategic position. Rather, I examine ways by which the United States can cope with new realities in the Third World as its member countries become more important international actors and wield greater power. This process of devolution is probably irreversible, and the United States has little choice but to accommodate it. Beyond that, however, it is also a process that could considerably benefit the United States if this country adjusts to, rather than ignores or opposes, change. The adjustment would not be easy, in either psychological or policy terms, for it must be made in ways that protect U.S. global and regional interests at a time when the devolution process is far from complete and its forms still fluid.

Imperial Interlude

The first step in coming to terms with the ambiguous U.S.–Third World situation is to understand how the United States has made such bewilderingly rapid transitions from near isolation to global leadership to a sense of malaise. As with most perceptions of change, the swings in U.S. power are by no means as extreme as imagined; the remembered past not so uniform in its composition. The late 1940s and 1950s were periods of great self-doubt for the United States—characterized by the Korean conflict, McCarthyism, missile gaps, and Khrushchev's threats—and our hands were not that steady. Nor was the United States fully a global power at that time. We learned in Hungary in 1956 that we lacked access to some areas. Our vast economic power was never applied globally. We never had coordinated, "imperial" economic policies, nor were our assistance programs ever on a scale that might raise the economies of new nations to levels compatible with our own. The illusion of U.S. omnipotence is largely a creature of nostalgia or, to those who wish to blame all the world's problems on the United States, of malice. Our role was special and remarkable, but it was within human dimensions.

Certainly for fifteen years or so after World War II, the United States enjoyed a historically unique global position that represented a sharp break from its past stance. If the European imperial powers had emerged stronger from World War II, the U.S. global role would have been very different; however, they were critically weakened by years of conflict and were no match for the tides of nationalism that the war had unleashed in Asia, Africa, and the Caribbean. The United States was caught up in the final stages of the imperial era and acted as the liquidator of a failing enterprise.[1]

The system of imperialism, in the broadest sense, ordered relations between several industrializing European states and the less advanced remainder of the world—essentially Asia, Africa, and Latin America—during the half century on either side of 1900. This was the first time that virtually the entire world was touched by a single set of relationships. Lines of control and domination extended from centers such as London, Paris, and Lisbon to the remotest corners of the world, without serious opposition from the colonialized peoples. British forces may have been wiped out at Kabul and Omdurman and the spectacular Sepoy Mutiny may have flamed across northern India, but these incidents were no threat to the imperial order. Such matters were soon put right with scarcely a ripple in the greater scheme of things.

The ease with which the countries of Europe dominated peripheral regions resulted mainly from the former's technological powers and to a lesser extent from their social organization. Most important, European countries were able to bring adequate military force to bear in any part of the periphery to ensure that no local force threatened the overall integrity of the imperial order. Surprisingly little force was needed; once the point had been made, colonial regions, innocent of nationalism, largely accepted the imperial relationships.

The arrangement persisted because both sides accepted it as inevitable, if not necessarily right. Because it was finely balanced mechanism, it needed only a push to make it collapse. The push came from the awakening of colonial nationalism and from the psychological and material impact of the Russo-Japanese and two world wars. The legitimacy of imperialism as a system was fatally undermined in both the colonies and the metropoles, and the process of recasting all elements of the center/periphery relationship was begun.

Relations among the imperial powers and a few bystanders (such as the United States) had been based on the principles of the balance of power—shared responsibility for global order among a number of nations, according to implicit but fairly well-understood rules. Since the states of the center reserved power for themselves, their relationships were superimposed on the rest of the world—including the Western Hemisphere where the Monroe Doctrine was born as a creature of the balance, not of unilateral U.S. action. The African and Asian periphery, which provided Europe with economic benefits as well as Indian and African troops in the world wars, figured into the power balance as extensions of their respective metropoles, not on their own behalf.

Like imperialism itself, however, international relations of the imperial period could not withstand the blows of two world wars. Former colonial powers not only lost their ability to dominate the rest of the world, but they were unable to uphold a structure that would protect themselves. Soon after World War II it became clear that there were to be only two decisive powers in the world—the Soviet Union and the United States. The United States, the stronger of the two, found itself in the role of conservator of the world order—and hence the heir of imperialism.

Americans have never thought of themselves as imperialists. Our modest colonial forays into the Pacific and Caribbean have hardly warranted such a grandiose label, and, in any case, they were reversed in the 1930s with the Good Neighbor Policy and provisions for Philippine independence. We in fact viewed ourselves as anticolonial and through much of the 1940s sided rhetorically with emerging nationalist movements. Moreover, the word *imperialism* has assumed a distinctly Leninist connotation in international discourse so that Americans categorically reject it as a term to describe their own experience or policies. Yet, when the United States found itself the leader of the residual imperial order after World War II, its leaders played their roles in ways that would have been well understood in ancient Rome or nineteenth-century London.

Like our British cousins, we acquired our empire in a fit of absentmindedness, but we did it suddenly and without any particular idea of how to dispose of the embarrassing acquisition. In Latin America and the Middle East, some economic benefits accrued to the United States in ways that correspond to classical theories of imperialism, and we incurred costs equally typical of the imperialist experience. However, it would be a misreading of history to assert that the United States sought out an imperial role or that its behavior could be explained in the essentially economic terms that define imperialism in the Leninist sense. In a pattern that was to dominate U.S. policy over the following decades, we took on the imperial heritage for reasons that had relatively little to do with the colonial areas or our direct interests there.

Our fiduciary concern was twofold—protection of our close allies in Europe and protection of an entire international system. The colonial peoples had been involved in global politics only as adjuncts to the contenders in the traditional balance of power, and we assumed that after independence they would play an analogous role, as adjuncts to one or the other side of the East-West competition. This was no idiosyncratic U.S. perception. Power distribution was in fact bipolar, and the U.S. perception of the Soviet Union as both evil and aggressive was widely shared. Stalinist Russia was a terrible place, and, even if the Soviets were unable to foment world revolution, their propaganda was frightening enough. Our leadership role was thus widely accepted: We had no rivals within our newly acquired empire, and the component parts did not seem restive. The persistence of a center/periphery relationship seemed logical.

The United States assumed its responsibilities for global management with appallingly little preparation.[2] Aside from some shallow familiarity with China and Latin America, we saw the colonial regions through the eyes of the metropole powers. Hence our approach to the colonies and new nations was triply flawed.

1. It was conditioned by a geopolitical approach that accorded overwhelming priority to our global competition with the Soviet Union.

2. It reflected our primary interest in those nations most important to us, a number of which were former metropole powers; we absorbed not only their view of the colonial regions but also supported some of their policies (notably those of The Netherlands in Indonesia, France in Indochina, and Portugal in India and Africa).

3. It was based on poor information about the situation in Asia and Africa so that, even with the best of intentions, we were bound to make grievous mistakes in dealing with the emerging nations.

In addition, we found that we had plunged into a new international situation that no one was equipped to understand—not we, the Europeans, the Marxists, nor the emerging nations themselves. The international order had embarked on a wrenching, revolutionary course that created scores of new international actors and made much previous experience irrelevant. Not only was our ship leaky, it was on uncharted seas, and we were scarcely aware of either fact, being new in the role of captain.

Some drastic errors of navigation resulted in a certain amount of wreckage to the small craft in our armada. Ultimately, our greatest error—our policy in Vietnam—was to cause us grievous damage as well and leave us with some dangerously gaping holes. Generally, however, we easily survived the collisions. World War II had left us with immense power and wealth, and we were in the enviable position of being able to afford even fairly serious mistakes without sustaining mortal damage.

Throughout the 1950s the United States had maintained an effective position of leadership based on capabilities that were not only unique but seemingly limitless. We were aided by good luck, mostly resulting from the inept Soviet policy, and generous doses of altruism and noblesse oblige made the burden of our leadership relatively palatable. We saw our role in very American terms: To whom much is given, much is demanded (and vice versa). We expected loyalty and were prepared to pay for it with heroic and demanding sacrifices up to and including the threat of nuclear war. We undertook our responsibilities with what we now recall as quiet strength and determination (the cowboy image is unavoidable).

Our errors were mainly the result of preoccupation with the threat posed to the new states and old colonies by the Soviet Union and China. This concern was not unfounded, for not only were the avowed goals and tactics of the Soviet Union (and, increasingly of China) threatening, but the new nations had no previous experience in making decisions about their own international roles. We overestimated, however, the capabilities of our adversaries and underestimated the ability of the newly independent states to make intelligent choices about their own futures. The rigidities of the bipolar structure masked a steadily increasing diversification and diffusion of power. The pressures of bipolarity also affected the moral and political quality of our policies. Though many U.S. policymakers were largely motivated by laudable, humanitarian concerns, the anticolonialist and democratic impetus of their policies was too often offset by support, or at least toleration, of unsavory regimes and a willingness to uphold the obsolete, colonial pretensions of their European allies.[3]

This odd mixture of strengths and weaknesses came into full flower during the presidency of John F. Kennedy. No other president before Jimmy Carter had as much interest in the Third World nor as great plans for constructive work there. Kennedy, however, was also driven by exaggerated concern over Khrushchev's largely rhetorical support for wars of national liberation, and, in his unilateral proclamation of the Alliance for Progress, Kennedy showed that he too was a captive of the "America knows best" approach to new nations.

The Camelot metaphor of the period was truer than many Americans appreciated. The Kennedy presidency produced genuine, if paternalistic, noblesse oblige—a knight errant to the distressed of the Third World in the person of Chester Bowles and even a sort of Round Table in the Peace Corps. At the same time, however, the debilitating forces of the Vietnam war and our vulnerabilities on the international economic front began to cut away the foundations of undisputed U.S. world leadership. Our involvement in Vietnam and the domestic crises of the Johnson and Nixon years created an atmosphere of self-doubt and saw a near breakdown in U.S. policy. The previous foreign-policy consensus (based largely on nonparticipation by most of the population) dissolved into a cacophony of public response when choices were made or proposed.[4]

The decline of consensus and rise in public questioning of U.S. foreign-policy leadership have greatly affected our relationships with other countries, particularly with those in the Third World. The results have been mixed. Greater reluctance to take on the dangers of military encounters; doubts about the wisdom of intervening in the affairs of others; wider acceptance of the fact that others have their own priorities; recognition that other policy imperatives exist besides besting the Soviet Union—all are undeniably sources of the much-lamented weakening of U.S. national will. Without question, these have at times hamstrung sensible policies that are important to the very preservation of a society that can permit itself the luxury of rethinking old prejudices. But the United States that demonstrates this greater breadth of understanding, humanity, and sensitivity is better equipped to deal with some realities of international relations that may appear less pressing in the short run but are ultimately real and important.

Domestic economic issues have also created ambiguities in U.S. global policies. Decline in our international competitiveness has resulted in part from important quality-of-life concerns. Conscious and successful U.S. foreign economic policies have set in motion a process that (although we may wish we knew how to slow down) has aided the rise of foreign competitors. The decline in U.S. economic fortunes in the 1970s caused Americans to doubt whether we should—or even could—carry our global burden indefinitely. Looking not only at Vietnam but also at other apparent failures (such as the inability of many U.S. Third World aid programs to produce political stability or sustained economic growth), many Americans rejected extensive involvement in affairs that they did not readily perceive as of great interest to us and in places where we had had at best mixed success. Some Americans even came to believe that U.S. assistance and involvement were intrinsically harmful.

U.S. foreign-policy leadership bears a significant share of the blame for this decline in public support. U.S. global involvement had been set forth largely in terms of opposition to the Soviet Union and, for a while, China. Often enough our policies had little rationale beyond this. As this logic flagged and as the failure in Vietnam became more evident, many citizens decided that the mandate of heaven no longer rested on Washington. The public joined in denouncing the apparently mindless globalism behind U.S. policy.

Obviously the critique was less than fair. The United States had no realistic alternative to global involvement. The very critics of globalism on security terms were often the most vociferous advocates of aggressive globalism on new issues. Americans deal in the coin of globalism, whether pressing for human-rights observance in South Africa or relating a Namibia settlement to the withdrawal of Cuban troops from Angola. It is a coin with two sides: On one side is a reasoned and responsible recognition that if certain desirable things are to be done in the world, the United States will have to play a major role, but on the other side is a proclivity to intervene in other countries' affairs on the assumption that the United States knows best. Globalism is an unavoidable part of U.S. foreign policy, and, though the degree of emphasis can be debated, a combination of world events and the American style leaves us with little choice but to deal with this reality as best we can.

2.
NEW CLAIMANTS FOR POWER

The Soviet Union

The collapse of the policy consensus within the United States is in retrospect hardly surprising. Not only the United States, but the world in which we were living, had changed and altered the premises of that consensus. The most noticeable change appeared in our relationship with the Soviet Union. In the first postwar decades, the bipolar reality meant that politics had become truly global, dangerous, and pressing. The greater flexibility of the multilateral balance of power was gone, and events anywhere in the world could potentially play back into a bipolar rivalry that still had to find a basis for avoiding cataclysmic war. Any event anywhere seemed politically significant, and the revolution in communications ensured real-time knowledge in all world capitals. The U.S.-Soviet competition was pervasive and overshadowed almost all relationships between the superpowers and the developing countries, and even the relationships among the latter. Polarization was an unavoidable fact of life in the postwar world, and the United States had no realistic alternative; global responsibilities were unavoidable.

Such tight bipolarity, however, cannot be sustained over time because it fails to accommodate the great diversity and potential for change in the international system. As long as the Soviets remained repellent and unapproachable, there was little prospect for a break in the pattern. However, the conditions of engagement between ourselves and the Soviets changed considerably in the mid-1950s.

Although the Soviet system remains objectionable in a number of respects, it underwent tremendous development in the post-Stalin years. Terror ceased to be the means of government and paranoia its guiding principle. The Soviet Union opened its borders to visitors, embarked on international-relations efforts of some sophistication, developed skills in objective assessment of foreign affairs, extended a modest amount of foreign aid, launched *Sputnik,* and began to take on the aspect of a nation that could be dealt with in traditional terms. Many people in the United States were skeptical of these changes—and wisely so, for they are easily reversible—but sometimes we failed to adequately appreciate the change in Soviet reality. In the eyes of others, especially in the Third World, the Soviet Union has adequately liberalized its political system and has generally comported itself on the international stage in acceptable ways. Given the standards of many Third World states, however, these criteria are not very rigorous. Moreover, the unedifying spectacle of U.S. domestic politics and international behavior in the late 1960s and early 1970s provided a welcome opportunity for Soviet apologists to discredit a more demanding standard of comparison. Though we may rejoice that the Soviet Union is behaving more humanely to its citizens and toward the outside world than it did under Stalin, the improvement of the Soviet image weakened one of the most convenient and most compelling rationales used by U.S. leadership.

The bipolar structure suffered another, more fundamental blow at the hands of Nikita Khrushchev. In the early postcolonial period, Soviet capabilities and presence in the developing areas were virtually nil, and Stalin's hard-line assumed that any new, non-Communist nation was automatically part of the camp of imperialism. Jawaharlal Nehru and others had proclaimed nonalignment, but the possibility for a Third World to emerge came only when Khrushchev enthusiastically jettisoned Stalinist orthodoxy and accepted the fact that nations could be nonaligned, thereby creating political options by which countries like India, Indonesia, Ghana, and Brazil could break out of the bipolar mold. Nonalignment was added to the otherwise bipolar scene, positing a new range of problems and opportunities for U.S. and Soviet policy. The global format of the present era was largely complete (the emergence of an independent China has not changed the basic terms), and the task of interrelating the bipolar superstructure and the increasingly multipolar substructure of international politics became the main day-to-day policy preoccupation.

Khrushchev's ambitions were grandiose and ambitious.[1] Through ideological sleight of hand the irrepressible Soviet leader sought to virtually define nations such as India into the Soviet camp; a modest surplus of resources enabled him to compete with U.S. foreign-aid projects through Soviet spectaculars, which were often of questionable economic value; and he ultimately outflanked the United States by establishing a military relationship with the Soviet Union's first "conquest" in the Third World—Cuba. Though all these activities caused consternation in the West and aroused a sense of pleasant excitement in the new nations, most fell flat. Khrushchev's successes in helping Third World nations lessen their Western ties rarely resulted in close ties to the Soviet Union, a point not clearly perceived by Western nations. His political and ideological maneuverings bore little fruit, and the Soviet debacle in the Cuban missile adventure illustrated that Moscow was unable to contest militarily against the United States in the Third World. If the Soviet Union were to play an effective role as a global superpower among the newly independent countries, it could not do so on the cheap.

Khrushchev's "harebrained" adventures in the Third World figured in his downfall, and his successors learned from his experience. Leonid Brezhnev and Aleksey Kosygin, both methodical and conservative men, quietly buried Khrushchev's enthusiasms and sharply lowered the Soviet profile in the Third World, which, coincidentally, was going through a conservative phase. The Soviets kept their options open and concentrated instead on new, costly, and slowly emerging policy initiatives necessary for the Soviet Union to contest globally with the United States. The first requirements were military: a strategic weapons capability that would offset U.S. superiority so vividly displayed in 1962, and air and naval capabilities for distant operations that could contest U.S. supremacy over a much wider area of the world.[2]

An early sign of success on the nuclear/strategic front was the negotiation of a SALT (Strategic Arms Limitation Talks) agreement on the basis of essential parity. First fruits of the distant operations buildup became evident in 1969, when the Soviet navy conducted operations in the Indian Ocean and Moscow played an important role in supporting North Vietnam. Soviet distant operations capabilities were (and remain) greatly inferior to those of the United States, but an important part of the gap has been closed. It was narrowed even farther as Vietnam sapped U.S. strength and the country's determination to play the dominant role in the developing world. Throughout the 1970s, our reluctance to use available instruments of force grew steadily. Indeed, the Soviets were probably surprised at how quickly they attained a position from which to challenge the United States. By the mid-1970s, they were able to support Cuban intervention in Angola, and their impressive worldwide naval exercises—backed by nuclear parity—demonstrated both that the USSR was able to enter the global lists on a basis that the United States could no longer disregard with impunity and that even such distant Soviet clients as Angola or South Yemen did not need to overly fear U.S. military pressure.

New Third World Nations

Though changes in relationships between the United States and the Soviet Union have been immensely important and have attracted great U.S. attention, changes in the Third World have been hardly less important and have perhaps even greater historical significance. The proliferation of national entities ranging from huge, hyperstable India through coup-ridden Ghana to miniscule but troublesome Grenada has made international relations infinitely more complex. If Third World membership is put at about 130 nations, there are mathematically 8,385 possible interactions among them, any of which could concern the United States. Few of these present the kind of vital problems that we encountered in relationships with Canada, Japan, the Soviet Union, or our European allies, but many have potential for causing significant problems to some segment of our society, for creating dangers in our relations with the Soviet Union, or for shaking some part of an already fragile international order.

Although the United States first thought of Third World nations as parts of a periphery that would automatically line up to support one or the other superpower, it had to rethink that concept when they embraced nonalignment in the late 1950s and 1960s. Even then the United States saw the Third World mainly as a passive object of international relations in which the United States and the Soviet Union would compete for support or even control of various parts. Large areas of the political map resembled those of the nineteenth century that had been left blank and labeled "unexplored" or "unclaimed," later to be tinted red, purple, or brown to represent new allegiance to a colonial power. Our conceptual maps did not reflect lack of exploration but still noted large unclaimed territories that would in due course be colored blue, red, or perhaps yellow, depending on the outcome of cold-war skirmishes.

The existence of a nonaligned movement was irksome to the superpowers, but neither felt (correctly, as it turned out) that its organization would have a significant, lasting effect on their relationships. The institutional failure of the nonaligned movement to make itself felt in the international system does not mean, however, that the nonalignment of individual nations was without significant impact on the global structure. By standing aside from U.S.-Soviet rivalry and occasionally exploiting it for their own advantage, Third World nations had an effect that was by and large helpful. At some sacrifice to international predictability, the nonaligned nations provided useful buffers between the two contending superpowers.

Similar to Queen Elizabeth I, the new nations were not content with international roles of playing off suitors against each other while maintaining the fiction of political virginity. Many wished to develop their strength against regional rivals, and a few, such as Brazil and India, aspired to broader international roles. For whichever reason, they began to develop national power in the ways that most nations have used after attaining independence.[3] This development continued quietly for a number of years, often abetted by the superpowers, who misperceived Third World military buildups. The superpowers measured them only in terms of their own capabilities or viewed them as modest accretions of support for their own positions in the global rivalry. No Third World state has developed power comparable to that of the two superpowers, but in their own contexts, a number of these nations have significant and even decisive military capabilities. Cuba has shown that, with a little help from friends, a Third World nation can project power over a distance and play a noticeable global role. Certainly the military forces of India, Nigeria, and Vietnam are capable of shaping political events in their immediate neighborhoods and even farther afield, as long as no superpower is determined to stop them.

These Third World powers can make their military might felt beyond the limits of smaller nations. The new military capabilities of large Third World states have decisively altered the old imperial premise that the states of the global center could impose their will on any part of the global periphery. Indisputably, either superpower could impose its will on any Third World country (or anywhere, for that matter) if it were undeterred by the other, if it went to maximum military mobilization, and if it convincingly held open a nuclear option. Each of the three conditions is highly doubtful, however, and the combination is unlikely beyond any reasonable odds. Major Third World states can no longer easily be physically coerced unless they are more or less adjacent to one of the superpowers and hence geographically accessible and probably not unless they are seen as within that superpower's sphere of influence.

U.S. failure in Vietnam demonstrated that even a middle-sized Third World state willing to commit the necessary resources for military development can fend off a major military effort by a distant superpower. Stronger Third World countries can now deploy extensive military capabilities backed by intense nationalism. If, hypothetically, the Soviet Union or the United States were to attack a distant country such as Brazil or India, the outcome of a conventional conflict would be doubtful and the task of occupation and pacification probably impossible. This proposition was not disproved by the Argentine debacle in the Falklands, for aside from the particular ineptitude of Argentine military leadership, the Falklands represented a distant operations problem for Buenos Aires as it did for London. Had the Falklands been contiguous to Argentina, the outcome would have been different.

Psychological factors are also important to military considerations. Armies tend to fight more tenaciously in defense of their homeland than in seizing foreign empires. At least the United States and European countries are rapidly losing the sense of mission and superiority necessary for imperial conquest and rule, and international opinion in general staunchly opposes such adventures. Even the Soviets are not immune to these trends, as witness their preferred use of Cuban proxies in Africa to direct intervention and their campaign in Afghanistan, which, by Soviet standards of applied massive force, is fairly half hearted.

The old center/periphery relationship no longer exists for military force, and, since power remains the ultimate determinant of the international order, for most other interactions as well. This change has immense implications for the foreign policy of all nations, including that of the two superpowers, but it has scarcely been perceived by the U.S. public or by many leaders of public opinion. Most Americans comfortably believe that a whiff of grapeshot would bring recalcitrant Gulf Arabs back into line on oil production matters or that a small, exemplary military mission could set things right in Central America. The realities of the new situation are not lost on the U.S. military. Complaints about lack of readiness, inadequate forces, and the like are the military's time-honored way of increasing their appropriations. However, current worries about the inadequacies of rapid deployment forces for combat in the Gulf or warnings about the levels of force that would be needed in Central American operations are deadly serious. Asymmetries of power still exist, but, in terms of relevant power, the situation has changed significantly to the advantage of Third World countries.[4]

The U.S.-Soviet rivalry gives the illusion of a private quarrel pursued in even the remotest corners of the world, with little regard to bystanders. An effect of U.S.-Soviet competition, however, has been to enhance the position of Third World countries. The ability of the Soviet Union to move large numbers of Cubans over a long distance to Angola in 1975 put the United States on notice that another country could also intervene physically in a distant place and to do so unchallenged. U.S. ability to manage the Congo in the 1960s operations could not be duplicated fifteen years later, just as U.S. military involvement in Lebanon in 1983 was a very different experience than that in 1958.

The reverse of the proposition is even more valid because the Soviet capabilities are still far behind those for U.S. distant operations, explaining in part the use of Cubans to introduce an ambiguity to complicate U.S. responses. The drift toward enhanced distant operations capabilities is inexorable, however; the Soviets will no doubt seek parity in that area with the same relentlessness that they have at the strategic level, and there is no inherent reason why they cannot achieve it. As in the strategic equation, balance is the logical outcome as long as neither side abandons the contest. The United States and the Soviets do not need to use decisive force against each other, only a deterrent that will serve to limit each other's actions, and the range of possible deterrents that we may use for that purpose is quite broad. This does not mean that we will always be restrained from using military force in the Third World. In situations in which one side convincingly argues that its vital interests are at stake, the other is likely to stand back lest the conflict escalate, and a few parts of the world are effectively inaccessible to either superpower.

Under foreseeable circumstances, all of these factors—U.S.-Soviet parity, psychological aspects in world opinion, and especially the change in power relationships between the former center and periphery—mean that in security terms at least, large pieces of the Third World are moving away not only from colonialism but also from subservient positions in the global order.

Naturally, Third World countries remain intensely vulnerable—especially in regard to their economies. The United States, the countries of Western Europe, Japan, and (in a very few cases) the Soviet Union have the economic power to do more damage to Third World countries than military attack could ever accomplish. Yet even here the balance has shifted somewhat. The United States can no longer collect its international debts at the point of a gun; nationalization of corporations is an accepted international practice; political manipulation of aid remains possible but is in bad repute; and, while the "South" of the international economic bargaining relationship cannot force its ideas of a new economic order, the "North" no longer unilaterally sets the terms of engagement. Even though all but the weakest Third World countries can assert a considerable degree of freedom on the international scene, some larger Third World nations and groups of nations are, in the technical parlance of international relations, no longer objects dominated by greater forces but subjects in their own right. In their neighborhoods and even farther afield, they no longer play the role of clients or proxies of the great powers but of nations with their own interests and capabilities. They cannot enact their new role against the will of both superpowers, but, as the case of Iran demonstrates a middling power can take the offensive against one superpower without becoming subservient to the other.

The emergence of new power centers in individual states and groups of states has considerable positive potential, but there are some definite minus signs in the overall account. Central direction and responsibility for global affairs are not necessarily bad, especially in a world in which individual nations have become so intensely independent and in which consensual forms of organization are so weak (a result in no small part of the behavior of the superpowers). Thus, to take the most urgent example, though both the United States and the Soviet Union are devoted to the globally useful goal of nonproliferation, they have been unable to convince nations such as India and Israel to support an international nonproliferation regime. The superpowers have also lost most of their ability to act, singly or jointly, in snuffing out regional conflicts that risk dangerous escalation. Too many Third World actors, such as India, Vietnam, Syria, and Israel, have become autonomous or so important to their superpower patrons that the cost to the superpower of blocking the client's pursuit of its perceived vital interests would be too high.

The three trends that we have been discussing—changes in the international order and the decline of effective U.S. power, the Soviet Union's progress toward global parity, and the development of centers of strength among the new nations—are interrelated and generally reinforce one another, as the following examples illustrate.

1. In Central America, the decline of U.S. leadership (either in terms of capability or will) intersects with a Cuban assertiveness underwritten by the Soviet Union and with the development of regional autonomous actors, such as Mexico and Venezuela, which are determined to take part in events in a hitherto North American preserve.

2. In Southeast Asia, a redefined U.S. role coincides with the appearance of the Soviet Union as an increasingly important factor in the regional power balance and with the development of two power centers—Vietnam and ASEAN (Association of Southeast Asian Nations)—intent on achieving the local outcomes that they prefer rather than those of the patron upon whom they nonetheless feel free to call for support.

Before pursuing this kind of specific analysis of the Third World and its interaction with U.S. policies, however, we need to consider how that analysis (and the policy that flows from it) can best be organized.

3.
GLOBAL AND REGIONAL SYSTEMS

The Rise of Regional Subsystems

The Third World is too vast and its member nations too diverse to be a useful unit of analysis, and the multiplicity of the Third World countries render it nearly useless as an object or subject of policy. Obviously, certain states play roles that command individual attention (we shall return to them later), but for several reasons the most useful approach to the Third World in general is by groupings of individual states.

1. There are very few security matters that can be treated in a purely bilateral context, especially in relations between the United States and Third World nations. For instance, we cannot deal with Thailand, Kenya, Morocco, or Venezuela without considering their regional contexts.

2. Third World countries tend to regard themselves as parts of regional contexts, whether Afro-Asia, the Organization of American States (OAS), or the Organization of African Unity (OAU) in the early days, or more recently smaller and more functionally specific groupings. If we fail to see them as they see themselves, we miss an important part of reality.

3. It is simply not possible in concept or in practice for any policymaker to deal with more than 100 new nations or even the independent governments of Africa or the Caribbean. Regional groupings are one way of aggregating them so that they fit into a workable scope. Admittedly, important detail will be lost but less than through a global or generalist approach.

4. A regional focus is important to the country specialist as a step toward enlarging perspectives and as a meeting ground on which to converse intelligently with the generalist.

The scholarly literature on regionalism is voluminous, but little of it is relevant for the particular purposes of this book.[1] It tends mostly to approach the issue in the peace-in-pieces context, often suggesting that regional structures such as the OAS, the OAU, ASEAN, and the Caribbean-Central American Common Market (CARICOM) may develop along the lines of the European Community (EC). The EC is in fact the implicit model for most regionalists; it has gradually progressed from tentative economic cooperation to a considerable degree of political consensus that has removed it from the lists of "troublesome" regional sources of international conflict. The EC, however, is not a very relevant model for the Third World, just as the Marshall Plan is largely irrelevant to the kinds of effort needed for economic development, for Europe has a much longer history of international interaction and more advanced institutions.

Scholarly literature is also concerned with the structures of regional groupings, reflecting the structuralist heritage of U.S. political thought. As with political activity in general, however, consideration of function is the most fruitful approach to regionalism. Not only is a functional approach more realistic, it also focuses attention on the dynamic nature of these groupings as they respond to specific challenges and sometimes show quite different composition or alignment in specific responses.

We come again to the question of terminology. The term *regional groupings* is not particularly elegant and carries with it static implications that suggest a degree of permanence and organization demonstrated by few individual groupings. The term is better suited to the structural school of thought from which it came and passed into the UN Charter as "regional arrangements." In this book we are interested in how regional groupings grow, how they perform their functions, and, especially, how they relate to the outside world. This *outside world* is the global system that embraces all international interactions and is currently characterized by the U.S.-Soviet competition and others' reactions to it. Just as the "global" system of the human body contains various subsystems (cardiovascular, muscular, skeletal) the international system is an amalgam of the overall global system and a series of subsystems subject to their own definition and description but able to function in their relationships with each other only within the context of the global system. As with the human body, the global system is more than the sum of its subsystem parts although it derives much of its meaning from them. (The global system could, however, do without Southeast Asia, for example, better than the human body could manage without a muscular subsystem.)[2] For the remainder of this study, I shall use the terms *subsystem, regional system,* or, when the context is clear, *system* in discussing these regional clusters.

Although some international subsystems (such as the North Atlantic system) are composed of far-flung members, those that we will consider tend to be geographically fairly compact. Since regional systems tend to be formed out of the interactions of their members, they usually consist of geographically proximate states that have greater opportunity to interact. Probably the kind of system that we are looking for in this study is not overly large. By focusing on function rather than structure we can beg the question of any subsystem's exact composition. Does Colombia belong to an Andean or Caribbean system? Is Afghanistan part of the Middle East or South Asia? In the context of function, the answer does not matter much and may actually change over time, according to the issue involved. Life itself is not that neat and tidy; neither will be our approach to defining specific regions.

Regional subsystems have two broad and inextricably related purposes. First, they regulate their internal affairs for their own collective, maximum benefit; second, they attempt to gain control of the conditions under which external systems (both the global system and other subsystems) relate to them. These purposes provide effective impetus in forming subsystems, rather than the efforts of outsiders, conscious attempts to build an economic union, or sweet rationality. Externally designed or imposed systems work only if, as in Eastern Europe or the Caribbean in earlier days, a major power extends forceful hegemony over a region. Such systems are unsatisfactory, however, because rather than resolving internal political difficulties, they only hold them in abeyance until the hand of control is removed. The Western European system is not in reality a success story growing out of economic rationality. Although economic structures such as the Coal and Steel Community were used as building blocks, the formative impulse of that system neatly illustrates my overall proposition. After World War II, European nations were convinced that conflict among themselves would destroy them and that they had to get their internal house in order by drawing Germany into a socializing network and by developing a common front against the grave external threat from the Soviet Union.

Conflict and ultimately its containment are the uncomfortable but inevitable preconditions of system formation, in at least equal measure with rational planning and negotiation.[3] Accepting the fact that "the boys have to fight it out to see who is the toughest on the block" is an unpleasant manifestation of realpolitik, at odds with the ethos of the international system. It could also be very dangerous: These conflicts could escalate to involve the superpowers and even the possibility of nuclear war. In most cases, the international community would want to snuff out conflict, and the United Nations' finest hours have come in precisely this area. Yet, one may ask, had the Pakistanis and Indians fought to a conclusion in 1948 and 1965, would the 1971 war have taken place? Have the frustration of the natural course of events in Cyprus over the years and the maintenance of an intrinsically untenable political situation in the eastern Mediterranean been a net plus for the international community or the people of Cyprus? Similar questions could be asked about the Middle East. A more open acknowledgment of Israeli and Syrian strength in Lebanon may, for instance, be the first step toward resolving conflict in that region, much as the 1973 war was a necessary step toward alleviating some of the difficulties between Egypt and Israel.

When the international community intervenes to stifle conflict, it should be aware that it may only be putting off the matter for a later and perhaps bloodier day, unless some nonviolent means can be found to promote stability and acceptance within the subsystem. Those prospects are rarely bright; few nations are likely to give up such a vital national aspiration as regional dominance or leadership, short of a convincing test at arms or force by a nation of unchallenged regional dominance. The system members will reach an agreement on power distribution only if it is more advantageous to all of them than any other arrangements might be to any of them or, more technically, when problem solving and autonomy are the subject of consensus and are higher values than political advantage, ideological commitment, or the particular outcome of any dispute.[4] The concept of autonomy (the ability of a system and its members to deflect intrusions from outside) brings us back to the second element important in system formation—external pressures.

One possible way that a subsystem can establish a better and more durable internal balance is to redefine itself and draw in a new member. The new member can do three things: provide a better internal balance if the region's problem was the presence of a large, powerful member; provide a pillar of strength around which the other members can rally for leadership and protection; or, if the new member was previously a threat to the system, bring a new element of tranquility and self-confidence. In a contemporary example, Indonesia's incorporation into ASEAN, provided the grouping with a strong central member and afforded the absorption of a previous threat. The particular problems posed by Vietnam and Cuba would also be most usefully resolved if these countries were included in neighboring systems.

Inclusion of an external threat, however, is more easily said than done, in part because of the relationships that these regional competitions have to the global balance between the United States and the Soviet Union. The most common and troublesome problem involved in the development of viable and autonomous regional systems arises when a member, unable to attain a satisfactory position within the system through its own strength, calls upon an outside power (generally a superpower or proxy) to become involved in the system.

Superpowers and the Global System

A logical relationship exists between superpowers and weaker or threatened members of a regional system. The latter want to resist the pretensions of a strong regional power that seeks hegemony, either through political means or through force. This provides the "pull" element of the relationship. The "push" is the superpower's desire to extend its influence into the subsystem—normal behavior for a nation with global aspirations. Generally this intrusion is justified not in the cause of frustrating the would-be hegemonic regional power but for reasons of the global balance, for example, U.S. need in the 1950s for allies to complete the ring of containment around the Soviet Union and China, which lent support to Pakistan for reasons connected to the cold war, or the Soviet response to Ethiopian requests for assistance in 1977, which permitted Moscow to establish new positions in the Horn of Africa. The logical extension of this situation is that the dominant regional power, seeing its position undermined by a superpower–lesser regional power alliance, would turn to the other superpower to counterbalance the initial intrusion. In the cases mentioned, India and Somalia did precisely this.

The result of these multiple intrusions is twofold: (1) The subsystem's autonomy is undermined; (2) regional and global disputes become intertwined so that pairs of allies are forced to take on the causes of their partners, whether or not they are particularly interested in them. The subsystem has then failed in one of its prime objectives—preservation of autonomy—and probably in the other as well because a system penetrated by the superpowers will not be able to organize itself effectively.

At first glance the regional situation would seem to be satisfactory to the superpowers for they have extended their influence into new areas, much as colonial powers had established positions of strength by playing off enemies in uncolonized parts of the world. The blessing is not unmixed, however; by associating with one contestant in a regional power balance, the intruding superpower risks losing its access to the other regional contestants and may find that the other superpower is invited into a region where it previously had no foothold. The superpower also may find itself responsible for the security and even the behavior of its client and thereby may acquire a commitment that can be costly if carried out—even costlier if later reneged on. Some material costs are also involved, although these are usually not too great. Prestige and far-flung commitments are inherent in the role of a superpower, and young, strong, and outward-thrusting nations bear these burdens with admirable stoicism. However, as the superpowers increase in age and experience, perhaps even wisdom, they develop doubts about their relationships with their client nations. These doubts probably begin to arise much earlier, even inside subsystems annexed to the global context, for the benefits expected by the superpowers never quite materialize. Ultimately the relationship may fall apart in recriminations because each party had different objectives in forming the alliance—a fatal difference unless the relationship can be reformulated on some new basis.

According to the traditional view, superpowers should have at least a veto right over the degree of autonomy available to regional subsystems because they alone have the global reach, decisive capabilities, support from relatively stable alliance systems, vast political influence, and ultimately, responsibility for the global order. The general interests and universal aspirations, which the Versailles conferees ascribed to great powers, should endow them with managerial responsibility not only for the global system but also for the subsystems to the extent that the latter's actions impinge on the global order. The superpowers should exercise this responsibility through cooperation in establishing and honoring some norms of behavior in dealing with each other and with third parties in circumstances that could affect the global order. They should limit regional conflicts that risk embroiling other systems and should, in the manner of Castlereagh or Bismarck, not become too closely identified with any subsystem member. Although in a regional dispute the strength of a globally weaker power may often be enhanced by its taking the side of a strong regional power, the superpower that has reached global parity should abstain from such a disruptive and potentially dangerous strategy. Superpowers also bear some responsibility for ensuring that their allies or clients—whether in the core alliance or within a subsystem—do not engage in activities inimical to the working of the global system.

Obviously, this description of the traditional superpower/regional client relationship has little to do with reality; over the past several years, the superpowers have been moving away from a cooperative approach to managing the global order and subsystem affairs. Although some of this change of course may be attributed to malevolence or ineptitude, the world of Versailles is long gone, and being a superpower is an increasingly difficult role to play. Because of their global reach and interests, today's superpowers are confronted with many more decisions concerning an incredibly broad range of geography and issues. Various sources pressure them to exercise their leadership power by doing something, rather than by following a policy of masterful inactivity. In particular, they must at times take sides on issues that lesser powers may safely ignore. Also, given the universality of the global system and the new issues constantly arising ("new" both in the sense of new types of issues and of additional issues of older types), they are pressed to assume responsibilities hitherto not the province of the global balancers. The most important development, of course, has been the rise of the Third World itself, which has made it impossible for the United States and the Soviet Union to pursue the tight bipolarity that would make effective superpower dominance possible. The two countries have become competitors rather than co-wardens of the global system.

To a point, this decline in tight bipolarity is welcome. Bipolarity is an intrinsically unstable situation and probably was a historical anomaly that could not endure. Furthermore, little evidence suggests that the Soviet Union and the United States separately are particularly adept at organizing regional security and that they should be entrusted with the task.

Regional states and subsystems enjoy greater freedom of action, which means that they too should observe a certain code of behavior. First, they should not pose a threat to another system or to a superpower (a problem that has not yet arisen), and they should contribute to, not detract from, global stability and international order. Appropriate behavior for subsystems goes beyond not starting wars that may escalate; it means that they and their individual members should not seek to exploit East-West tensions in ways that could be destabilizing or inflame North-South security or economic problems, and that they should handle new global issues constructively and be open to the legitimate access of outside powers. At best the record of the regional nations in observing their set of commandments is only somewhat better than that of the superpowers.

The quintessential responsibility of a regional subsystem, however, is the preservation of its autonomy, a task that all regional groupings recognize but find extremely difficult within a dynamic and competitive global system. Autonomy is not an absolute condition, and it varies in degree. If we define it as a state or region's ability to keep outsiders from defining the issues that constitute the local agenda, the record in the Third World is not that bad and seems to be improving. A number of Third World states have been able to assert that level of autonomy effectively, albeit sometimes at considerable costs to their economies and their citizens' liberties. A number of regional subsystems show increasing skill at avoiding cold-war bipolarity as the organizing principle of their affairs and at curbing superpower intrusions into their systems.

The current international environment in fact is not wholly inhospitable to regional autonomy. Colonialism is dead, and because of the weaknesses of superpower management, the global system's ability to intrude has been considerably weakened. The "push" factor is further undermined by the fact that the international system frowns on overt aggression and occasionally even does something about it. Subsystem vulnerabilities result much more from the "pull" factor that arises when a nation mismanages its affairs and gives rise to an almost irresistible occasion for interference by one or the other superpower, to the detriment of the superpowers' relations and of the subsystem's autonomy. The most difficult challenge to regional subsystems is to manage conflict and security in their specific locales in ways compatible with the stable functioning of the global system.

To use an analogy,[5] subsystems should function as ethnic neighborhoods traditionally did in the big cities of the United States: Although internal politics were intense and sometimes violent, they were confined to the geographic limits of the neighborhood, and issues were ultimately settled by the neighbors themselves. Gangs did not roam uptown to do their fighting, and if the outside arbiters (the police) were called in, the system had failed and the neighbors themselves felt disgraced. The arrangement was not always pretty and justice might or might not have been done, but the terms of engagement were clear. From the viewpoint of municipal governments with limited resources, functions, and legitimacy, the arrangement was highly satisfactory. When a genuine competition took place for the spoils of a municipal office, ethnic leaders had a particularly good chance of enhancing the autonomy of their turf by maneuvering between competing political parties. This somewhat nostalgic picture has more than a few similarities to the current international scene. The global municipality is certainly short of resources and legitimacy, global parties compete and can be played off against each other, and, as the example of much of Africa suggests, the regions are willing to tolerate considerable internal injustice before calling in the global cops.

Regional Influentials in the Third World

Besides superpowers and regional subsystems, another class of actors is important to the future of the Third World in general and to regional subsystems in particular. We have already noted that some nations near or within subsystems have substantially greater strength than do their neighbors and aspire to a larger role, either as the dominant member of the system or as a power whose role is recognized as transregional, if not global. This may merely mean that some nations are stronger than others, with strength being a key element in international relations. Yet an additional important and dynamic element is in the picture; a number of these nations consciously seek to restructure the global system in their favor. We are familiar with this phenomenon in the economic sphere; in international economic councils, oil-rich Arabs have staked out a place for themselves that rivals that of many more established European powers. Newly industrialized countries as well seek to change some rules of the world trading system to their advantage though the General Agreement on Trade and Tariffs (GATT).[6]

Nehru's India was the first of such nations to assert its claims, relying on moral suasion and diplomacy. When this approach came up against the hard realities of the Peoples' Liberation Army of China in 1962, Nehru's successors realized that they would have to earn their position the hard way—through military strength—and have made a convincing job of it. Indonesia's Sukarno sought his moment in the sun as the would-be leader of the New Emerging Forces but ran afoul of domestic realities. His successors have, at least for the time being, sublimated Indonesia's aspirations through membership in ASEAN. Several African leaders, most strikingly Kwame Nkrumah, sought a role on the global stage but lacked a convincing base of operations. Like Nehru, these Africans sought status on the cheap; unlike India, they could not fall back on national strength when their bluff was called. Claims to international status must be backed up in traditional terms of power, whether a country is a superpower or a regional power. The international community does not recognize any other currency, UN one-nation-one-vote procedures notwithstanding.

The roster of regional influentials is fairly predictable and generally based on size, population, economic development, and other tangible criteria, although intangibles such as leadership, ideology, and national will are required to activate this potential. Nations such as India, Nigeria, or Brazil almost inevitably play substantial roles in the post-colonial world, as long as they do a tolerably decent job of keeping their domestic affairs in order. Some share of the pie has to be doled out to them if world power distribution is to reflect reality and have some prospect of stability. The allotment process, however, is excruciatingly difficult because in the power pie, unlike in the economic pie, a country or region's relative share is important and someone else has to give up some part of its share if the distribution is to be more equitable. The matter is complicated by the Soviet Union's bid for a major realignment of power at the global level. Since the United States has held by far the largest slice of this pie in postwar years, it is not difficult to see the direction in which all these claimants are casting their eyes.

The problems that regional influentials can cause for the global system are minor compared to the impact that they can have on their neighbors. The regional influential would make its initial claims in terms of the lion's share of the slice of the power pie available to its subsystem. This has been the experience of countries around Iran; Central Americans will find that trading the United States for Mexico brings its own set of problems. In fact, any system built on political realities—and only such systems have any hope of survival—would find that some of these realities are uncomfortable or even unacceptable when explicitly stated.

The bargain is not without its benefits, however: A regional subsystem without a prominent, leading member lacks a nucleus around which to coalesce, a compelling spokesman, and, ultimately, an element of strength that would be important if the system were to come under direct attack from outside. A weakness of the Front Line state grouping in southern Africa is the absence of any such coalescing force. Ironically, the Constellation of States idea propounded by South Africa would fit the bill nicely since the Republic of South Africa is just the kind of focal point around which a regional system could coalesce, were it not for the republic's peculiar institution. A majority-ruled South Africa will, of course, be quite a different matter. From the viewpoint of a powerful member, a position of explicit or implicit leadership within the subsystem would help validate its claims to international status. As India has found, failure to come to terms with the local environment is costly in terms of broader aspirations.

At best it is a chancy proposition whether a regional influential will develop a relationship with its neighbors that is stable and useful in terms of the international order. The country must both be domesticated (cease being threatening) and be provided with a satisfying role in relationship to the system. The North American system required about a hundred years to domesticate the United States and to learn to live with U.S. primacy. Mexicans are not sure that the process is complete even now. The existence of an acknowledged regional leader can be very useful to other members of the international system, but if the United States were to relate only to these nations, it would miss important opportunities with other subsystem members and perhaps even undermine the viability of the subsystem.

Israel and South Africa have demonstrated that regionally influential powers can shape a subsystem by providing an external threat, and Vietnam and Cuba have done wonders for the vitality of ASEAN and the nascent Central American–Caribbean grouping. The threat, however, can also be destructive if it is not dealt with either by a Toynbean response from the regional system as a whole, disciplined by one of the superpowers, or by the deviant's absorption into the system. Clearly this latter alternative promises to be the most lasting, but it is also the most difficult to achieve.

Regional influentials present still another kind of problem: They are difficult to distinguish from their setting. Does West Africa, for instance, have any meaning in terms of power or politics aside from Nigeria? When we talk of South Asia we are usually so overwhelmingly concerned with India that other nations receive short shrift—even Pakistan, which in almost any other part of the world would be a major regional power. Mexico would define any Central American system, and an effective ASEAN is unthinkable without Indonesia.

When we discussed the shift of power from the old center to the formal colonial periphery, we were really concerned with regional influentials. Togo has not bettered its relative power position by much, nor has Uruguay. However, Nigeria and Brazil—even Argentina—have, because of both the general devolution of power away from the center and some generally well-thought-out acquisitions of military hardware. During the 1970s these countries have piled up hardware at an astounding rate, and several are poised to take the next step to nuclear status. They are making good their claim to recognition beyond their immediate regional setting by establishing a clear dominance within that setting.

Existence of bipolar parity—especially as it reaches outlying areas— means that strong regional powers would have less to fear from the disciplining hand of a superpower and could gain considerable freedom of action in dealing with their neighbors. They lose only if (1) the two superpowers begin to exercise a tight bipolarity or condominium that greatly restricts other actors or (2) one superpower withdraws, leaving the other free to exercise hegemonic control and to reverse the process of power devolution to the periphery.

Short-term trends in the growth of Third World countries' international importance could be interpreted to indicate a downswing in their prospects. Several countries that appeared to be on the verge of major international status in the mid-1970s are questionable prospects today. The collapse of the boom market in oil has dealt a blow to the pretensions of Nigeria (reinforced by bad management) and Mexico. The stagnation of the international economy in the late 1970s and early 1980s undermined the position of countries like Brazil that had relied heavily on exports, and it triggered a major debt crisis that sapped their self-confidence. OPEC and the Group of 77 today look much less formidable. A leadership failure in India diminished that country's stature in the nonaligned world and its ability even to lead South Asia. Although we are not considering China as a Third World country, it too looks much less impressive than it did a decade ago. Changes in Iran defy description. On the other hand, the United States has regained some of its self-confidence, sense of purpose, and even economic leadership at the expense of Western Europe as well as the Third World. The Soviet Union, meanwhile, has been going through a series of weak, elderly leaders, and its economy has continued to falter. The new Gorbachev regime has quickly dispelled the image of senility but has yet to demonstrate an ability to reinvigorate the USSR.

These changes could be interpreted as evidence that the situation in the 1970s was only an aberration and that relative relationships along the lines of those in the 1950s can and will be restored. This assumption, however, is just as erroneous as the exaggeration of comparative U.S. weakness in the 1970s. We are dealing with long-term trends: Ups and downs will occur on the graph lines, but these will only complicate— not change—the basic picture. Nations with such advantages as large resource bases, large populations, and important geostrategic locations will almost inevitably have impressive futures. Tocqueville's vision of the United States was not invalidated by the Civil War and the repeated economic setbacks in the nineteenth century. It is also not of great consequence whether one or the other regional influential turns out to have feet of clay. The emergence of the imperial world order was also not smooth, as one or another imperial power faded and economic crises threatened to undermine the entire system.

The global economic situation of the mid-1980s will also change. The economic position of the United States vis-à-vis Europe is not likely to be permanent. The oil market will again be tight. The Soviet Union may even succumb to economic rationality. Diffusion of science and technology will strengthen the economies of the Third World countries that learn how to exploit them. (Asian countries weathered the change in terms of trade in the 1970s quite well.) Debt crises will be resolved (and new ones will arise), and the international economy will in its own interest find ways for newly industrializing countries to gain a more appropriate share of world trade. Several have already made good progress in getting their houses back in order. The changing pattern in military power has hardly been affected by the economic downswing, and large populations in the Third World remain an element of strength as well as one of weakness. The United States itself has a well-documented record of wide shifts in its propensity for international involvement.

Determinism of any kind is a poor guide to the future, and prediction of specific changes is foolhardy—especially for the more distant future. Disregard of the lessons of history and refusal to recognize the general direction of change are, however, even more foolhardy for those charged with making policy for a nation's—and a world's—future. Such disregard is hardly less detrimental to wise policymaking for the short term. The existence of significant power centers in the Third World and the growing importance of the Third World as a whole are among the most compelling propositions facing U.S. policymakers. They are likely to be facts of life with which we must live from now on.

4.
RELATING
TO THE THIRD WORLD

The Need for Access

I have mainly discussed international relations in terms of U.S. capabilities and those of other countries. An equally critical element of the foreign-policy equation is the matter of interests. In a period of declining relative strength, the United States has been tempted to define its interests downward too rapidly in order to spare itself the effort of mustering capabilities to protect them, even when these capabilities are within reach. We approached Asia in this spirit in the mid-1970s, and some voices have urged us to write off even such vital responsibilities as our role in Europe, though it is within our capability to protect. The shift in national mood in the 1980s has righted the balance and correctly so; President Ronald Reagan is correct when he affirms that "no area of the world is beyond the scope of American interests." This swing in the attitudinal pendulum, however, needs to be carefully watched. It could go too far and involve the United States in the other misreading of the interests/capability relationship: The United States is even more likely to err by asserting nonvital interests to be vital or by asserting interests for which our capabilities are clearly insufficient. Such errors were not of great moment when we held an unchallenged ascendancy, but Vietnam marked the end of that era because it stretched our resources beyond our capabilities in support of an overvalued interest. Today, with a much smaller margin for error, we must calculate more accurately what we require, what we can afford, and what our prospects are for achieving our objectives.

In dealing with the Third World, these calculations should yield an encouraging answer, for U.S. needs can generally be summarized under the term *legitimate access*. Legitimate access entails routine diplomatic access to do things such as look after our citizens who have run afoul of local laws; economic access to maintain such economic relations as trade and investment on equitable terms; and ability to perform a plethora of routine but important tasks, such as ensuring overflight rights for our airlines. In addition, the United States needs political access to ensure that nonaligned countries consider (if not necessarily accept) its point of view on important questions on a most-favored-nation basis. Military access, aside from routine port calls or occasional landing rights, leads into more questionable areas, but we can legitimately expect that our access would be no less than that accorded to our rivals.[1]

Concern about an area does not solely depend on a country's interests. Level of concern is the product of interest times threat; even a vital interest that is threatened need not be the object of great attention or resource expenditure. U.S. dependence on oil from the Gulf states, for instance, is a matter of great concern because it is potentially threatened by both the regional states and the Soviet Union. *If* the Soviet Union were impotent or on the other side of the world from the Gulf *and if* we could apply decisive military force in the region *and if* the local states could not survive very long without their oil revenues, the Gulf would rightly be low on our list of concerns, subject only to occasional review. The threat to our access in Afghanistan or Laos is extremely high, but because we have few interests in those countries we do not need to be particularly concerned.

I noted in Chapter 3 that one quality that a Third World subsystem or individual state should have is the ability to determine autonomously its relationship with the outside world. Access is a function of autonomy, and like autonomy, it comes in degrees. The narrowly defined minimum previously outlined is just that, a minimum. Any member of the international community has the right to expect it, and problems usually arise only when a country demands access beyond this minimum. The United States enjoys substantially more than minimum access in most Third World countries and in some holds almost a preemptive position vis-à-vis the Soviet Union. For the most part, however, adequate degrees of access are available on a most-favored-nation basis. That would seem to be the essence of nonalignment. When the United States expects a certain level of access for itself, it cannot reasonably expect such access to be denied to others unless it is willing to pay a substantial price. Conversely, when we demand that nations limit the access that they grant to our rivals, we have to expect that they may likewise limit our own access. In earlier years we did make such demands, even protesting vigorously when some Third World nations accepted economic assistance from the Soviet Union, but as our preemptive capabilities have declined in more recent years, our common sense has grown.

Still, in some cases U.S. interests demand more than routine access. In addition to depending on Gulf oil, we cannot readily do without some minerals from Africa. Our bases in the Philippines may well be vital to our wider interests in the Southwest Pacific and Indian Oceans, and we demand some veto right over certain foreign-policy choices in nearby nations (e.g., granting of base rights to nations hostile to the United States).

In practice, there are very few areas in the world where access becomes a serious problem resulting from a combination of high levels of interest and of threat. Although some nations would prefer to have nothing to do with the United States, even these usually see their interests best served by granting the kind and degree of access that we need. The U.S. advantage rests in the fact that the country and its associates in Europe and Japan are much more attractive than is the Soviet Union, especially in economic terms. We have the technology and capital that Third World states—even Marxist nations such as Angola and Mozambique—need for development, and the Soviet Union does not. Almost no nation in the world could rationally forego economic relations with the United States whereas few have uniquely valuable economic relations with the USSR. Our cultural attraction is also stronger than that of the Soviet Union, especially at the popular level. Even though Soviet Union can enjoy all the freedom of access it wants in the Third World, in very few cases will it be able to use that access to compete effectively with the United States. In a few selected countries, Moscow might be able to muster economic resources (Vietnam and Cuba are cases in point), and in a few others the nature of the state economic system might provide openings for Soviet economic activity that Moscow could not acquire on its own.[2] India's state-directed economy, for instance, formed the basis for the large Indo-Soviet trade, but India looks to the West for help in economic development.

A still more significant advantage for the United States could lie in the differing U.S. and Soviet global roles. The Soviet Union has moved into an expansionist, neo-imperialist phase that inevitably entails political and ideological demands. Since the newly independent nations are concerned with limiting external intrusions, they should come into conflict with the Soviets to a much greater extent than with the United States because we are lowering our profile in most of the Third World countries and our needs are largely compatible with the desires of the new nations. Unfortunately, however, things do not always work out that way. The Soviets, who have developed no little skill in their diplomacy, have learned to pull back in the face of resistance. And regrettably, the United

States has too often made unnecessary or poorly thought-out demands on Third World countries, moving beyond legitimate access to intrusiveness. Most of these demands have been in the security area, but others have been equally intrusive in fields ranging from economic performance to nonproliferation. There is no arguing that some of these intrusive demands have been important to make; we cannot settle for minimum access in all areas and for all purposes. When we make them, however, we must be very sure that they reflect important priorities and are realistic in relation to our capabilities.

Intrusion and Intervention

Access can thus become intrusiveness and, in an extreme form, intervention. Indeed, a number of authors have seen interventionism as a hallmark of U.S. policy toward the Third World, and a substantial amount of literature has accumulated on this subject, much of it by Marxists or by those seeking to expiate the perceived sins of U.S. involvement in Vietnam. Although the U.S. predilection to dabble in the affairs of others has been very costly, much of the academic criticism of interventionism has very limited validity. The Marxist argument—that the United States intervenes in other countries to protect its economic interests—is not borne out in reality. There is a basic belief in the United States that the welfare of all peoples is best served by the kind of open economic system that has benefited our domestic economy and international trade. The available evidence suggests that this argument remains more valid than any other that has been offered as a realistic alternative. The United States remains interested in maximizing its gains from the world economy. Especially in early postwar years, Washington's rhetoric dwelled heavily on the supposed commercial benefits of an active U.S. role in regions emerging from colonialism.

In practice, little U.S. intervention can be ascribed primarily to economic motives. With the coming of the cold war, the rhetoric of economic gain largely disappeared, and the reality has faded with it. Although the United States was able to profit from its intervention on behalf of the shah of Iran in 1953, more recent concern with that area has involved U.S. economic interests in the area of economic security, not profit. Despite International Telephone and Telegraph's (ITT) bizarre foray in Chile, neither the U.S. government nor most corporations seem anxious to use force to protect foreign investments or to open up foreign markets. The multinational corporation that needs U.S. government involvement to advance its interests should probably look for a new set of corporate. officers.

When high-level policy councils in Washington seriously consider intervention, U.S. economic interests are among the first to be discounted. Security concerns are overwhelmingly at the heart of U.S. intervention, and second place is held by humanitarian and ideological motives. That mix of interests was evident in Vietnam, and it seems also to be present in our current involvement in Central America. Although one can argue in all these cases that U.S. economic interests would in the long run best be served by the triumph of our security interests and hence that intervention is economic in its fundamental motivation, few policymakers look that far into the future.

Another tenet of revisionist orthodoxy is that the United States has become so identified with Third World elites that it is bound to intervene to perpetuate their incumbency. This tenet is also largely a myth of the past.[3] Stated in a somewhat different form, however, the argument has strength. The United States may or may not look kindly on a given elite, but U.S. strong attraction to stability can easily result in preoccupation with the status quo and a tendency to support the group most likely to preserve it. Since the Soviet Union and other socialist states usually consider that their interests are served by a disruption of the status quo in countries where U.S. interests are entrenched, they look for possibilities for counterintervention. The effects of intervention, at the internal as well as intrasystem levels, can thereby lead to an undesirable expansion of global competition into the affected system.

Intervention as a general principle is morally neutral.[4] Specific instances of intervention can be judged by two criteria. The first criterion is subjective: Action to protect a friendly nation being bullied by a neighbor, mediation of disputes not likely to be resolved constructively by the parties themselves, and opposition to egregious human-rights violations by vicious regimes are laudable acts by virtually any standards. Those are the easy cases; subjective criteria are usually not very useful beyond the individual imputing them. After all intervention in Vietnam was conducted in part for a very high purpose, and most of those responsible believed that they were acting morally; yet in substantial contrary opinion the U.S. experience in Vietnam is seen as immoral in both its purpose and its execution.

The second criterion is narrower and somewhat easier to apply: Did the intervention advance U.S. interests (1) in the short run and (2) in the long run? A question implied in this criterion is whether the same or an equally acceptable outcome would have resulted if the United States had not intervened? Here again views differ. U.S. involvement in Vietnam bought time for other Southeast Asian states to consolidate their positions; thus, following our withdrawal, the rest of the regional states did not topple like the row of dominoes many outsiders had thought them to be. Nevertheless, it is impossible to argue that net U.S. interests were furthered by the Vietnam war, and the intervention must be judged a failure.

Another difficult case is the United States' 1953 intervention in Iran. It was certainly successful in its own terms: The shah regained the throne and the United States received economic and political benefits for nearly a generation after. Although the United States has paid dearly in the past several years for its association with the shah, a quarter century of benefits in a critical area probably qualifies this intervention as a success. In other instances, such as in the Dominican Republic and Lebanon (1958), it appears in retrospect that we could have achieved much the same results through diplomacy and saved ourselves considerable unpleasantness. Finally, some U.S. interventions were disastrous by any criteria. Cambodia was preeminent among these.

Intrusive involvement can also arise from well-meant efforts at mediation and peacemaking. The United States often becomes involved because of its relationship with one of the parties, but it is then called upon for mediation and other forms of dispute settlement in which it is not directly concerned. Sometimes our intention is nothing more than an effort to help others out of their difficulties; more frequently, however, we enter a dispute in the belief that its continuation would be harmful to our global concerns. Our global involvement, and our subsidiary assumption that conflict is a bad thing, opens up limitless vistas, and we risk sinking ever deeper into a dangerous quagmire. Over time, the expectation has grown that the United States will mediate practically anything anywhere, be it in Yemen or West Irian (in which a direct U.S. interest is hard to discern) or in the Arab-Israeli region or in southern Africa (where the interest is clear). Although it is flattering to be seen as a peacemaker, the wisdom of becoming involved is open to question when we do not have a major stake in the outcome of a particular dispute. We have spent vast amounts of energy and political capital on Lebanon, Cyprus, and Kashmir; at best we have little to show for our efforts and at worst we have become part of the problem ourselves. In Kashmir the issue became somewhat more manageable once we withdrew and the issue lost its cold-war color. As suggested earlier, conflict within an international subsystem, when worked out on its own terms, can sometimes serve to strengthen the system.

Despite the now fashionable aversion to intervention and the costs of pursuing interventionist policies, some intervention is moral and some is important for our national interest. Simplemindedly rejecting the idea of intervention or defining it as a motivation rather than an instrument of policy, as some writers have (to be able to pin a judgmental label on it), makes no sense, and many of these same critics would favor intervention on issues of their own choosing. For better or worse, the United States is condemned to an interventionist role because of its global calling. Much sport is made nowadays of such Lyndon Johnson quotations as "we did not choose to be the guardian at the gates but there is no one else."[5] However, no one else today, as in 1964, is able and willing to do some nasty jobs that need to be done—except for the Soviet Union, and it is rarely in U.S. interests or that of others to leave the road open to the USSR. Whatever doubts we may have developed in the United States over the past years about our own righteousness—and these doubts are often valid—we do nobody a serivce by equating ourselves with a regime that remains unjust and inefficient, as well as threatening.

Clearly this approach will not appeal to international lawyers who have developed some impressive and wise rules against intervention. Even some fine treaty provisions have been formulated on the subject. Intervention is a form of vigilante justice and, therefore, not acceptable to organized society. When inernational law becomes universally enforceable, unilateral intervention will be criminal and reprehensible behavior. Until then, however, it is part of any great nation's policy repertoire, just as vigilante justice was accepted as a necessary evil in the early American West.

Conflicting Pulls of Globalism and Regionalism

The American propensity to intervene in other nations' affairs to a great extent arises from our role as a superpower with global responsibilities. The failures of our interventions often result from insufficient attention to affairs at the subglobal or regional level. Since at least 1941 we have been conditioned to view our participation in international affairs in a global context, and we have come to understand the broad sweep of global issues better than the minutiae of regional affairs. Although this sort of globalism is reasonable for the United States, failure to gain comparable understanding of regional perspectives leads to serious problems in our policymaking.

- Our understanding is harmed by an inevitable overaggregation of Third World interests and characteristics.
- We lose much of our already limited capacity for politically nuanced policies toward specific countries and regions.
- Our policies become unpredictable and sometimes appear threatening to other countries, since we are operating from a script that they do not share.

- When regional affairs become invested with a global significance, they are blown out of any realistic proportion, a process difficult to reverse. (The internal affairs of Vietnam and Afghanistan inappropriately became lasting features of the global landscape because of the way in which we treated the former and the Soviets treated the latter.)
- Even more serious, an overly global focus can lead us to misinterpret regional events on the assumption that the rival superpower is behind purely indigenous developments.
- When regional problems are addressed in terms of global consideration, there is little prospect of those problems being definitively solved in their own terms and, hence, as supportive elements in the global picture. At best we can buy some time.
- Finally, a global focus in today's world misses most of the point, since the superpower confrontation is itself only a sterile stalemate. Effective politics take place in the regional systems where superpowers can compete for winnable stakes between themselves and with individual Third World countries.

As a superpower the United States makes excessive use of a global prism and expects others to adopt the same outlook, following the U.S. lead in pursuing common interests and shaping their policies. This attitude leads to excessive demands on Third World countries and an impression that our global stake in regional developments is greater than that of the regional states themselves. These corollaries put us at odds with regionally influential powers, and, when our views do prevail, regional states expect to extract compensatory benefits that we may not consider to be in our interest to provide.

Much of this critique of U.S. globalism is familiar to anyone who has dipped into the relevant literature,[6] but a less familiar, less often articulated school of criticism is directed against regionalists supposedly so preoccupied with their areas of specialization that they disregard U.S. interests in favor of those of their clients. Henry Kissinger came close to making this charge in his discussion of the presumed pro-India orientation of the Department of State in 1971,[7] and it is comforting to know that according to a corresponding body of opinion in India the Indian Ministry of External Affairs is unpatriotically pro-American. I have never met any U.S. (or Indian) official who puts the interests of a foreign country above those of his own nation, but a broader charge is not without merit. Regional specialists (rather more among academics than in government) view the world through their own narrow prism and frequently fail to acquire the broad grasp of policy priorities needed for relating local concerns to U.S. national interests. Unquestionably, one strength of the regionalists is that they more openmindedly assess the capabilities of the people with whom they are familiar than do the globalists, who, by and large believe that only China, among nations with a per capita gross national product of less than $500, is capable of making intelligent political judgments. Yet the regionalist may dangerously underestimate a client's vulnerability to outside threats.

Within the global preoccupation of the U.S. government are little pockets of thriving regionalism. Areas that have no apparent global significance are the happy preserve of regional specialists making small decisions on their own with little reference to the outside world. When the specialists' moment of truth comes, no conceptual link exists between their activities and the global outlook of U.S. leaders, and the regional networks of relationships that they have developed risk being blown away as irrelevant to the big picture. Neither set of interests is well served in this case, and all policymakers should be concerned to keep decisions about even obscure parts of the world well connected to the overall policy concept, even though this approach may not always yield the most comfortable short-term results.

The respective weaknesses in globalist and regionalist approaches can be serious, but they can be dealt with rationally if they are not cloaked in excessive rhetoric and mutual misrepresentation. In the minds of many ardent critics globalism became identified with the policies that involved the United States in Vietnam and with the realpolitik of Henry Kissinger. Amplified in the heated atmosphere of the early 1970s, these connections led to an equation of globalism with immorality and insensitivity, which not only missed the point of our intervention in Vietnam (which was nothing if not a crusade) but mistakenly related the globalism versus regionalism contest to a different debate over the role of morality in U.S. foreign policy. U.S. activities in Vietnam and Kissinger's approach to foreign policy are certainly valid subjects of concern in the traditional debate about morality, but forcing globalism and regionalism into that mold is a simple case of guilt—or innocence—by association. An equally false approach is to relate them to another long-standing discussion in U.S. foreign policy—isolationism versus involvement. Again, there are some parallels in that a globalist commitment cannot be reconciled with isolationism, but citing Washington's farewell address and holding up the sad example of U.S. failure to play a constructive role in the interwar period are not helpful in dealing with the matters at stake today. Important issues are involved in the tension between globalism and regionalism, and we are unlikely to arrive at an understanding of them by setting up distorted caricatures of Henry Kissinger and Andrew Young as straw men.

Differences between global and regional approaches should be seen not as elements of a polemic but as useful, dialectic concepts to help order our thinking and our policies. We must synthesize policies that meet the minimum requirements of these conflicting and persistent demands on us; policies that work from only one of the contending viewpoints will be inadequate. Undeniably, the global threat is more clear, present, and potentially catastrophic: If the United States does not prevent nuclear war, maintain its ability to resist nuclear blackmail, and support forces able to project power to protect far-flung interests, it will not have to worry about whether its regional policies are adequate, let alone be able to stand by friends who come under threat from Moscow and its allies. If the international economic situation collapses, we would hardly be able to strengthen the economies of our less-developed friends and allies.

Failure at the global level can be equally damaging to pursuit of "new issues" at the regional level. U.S. failure to reach strategic arms-control agreements (including a comprehensive test ban) with the Soviet Union in the late 1970s greatly undercut the legitimacy of our demands that nonnuclear states adhere to the Non-Proliferation Treaty. Similarly, by failing to reach agreement with the Soviets and our European allies on limiting conventional arms transfers, we had no credible basis upon which to approach the developing countries to restrain their purchases.

Yet failure to meet the challenges posed by regional problems can be almost as harmful to the U.S. global posture as failure at the global level.[8] If we were to alienate the bulk of regionally influential countries, this would certainly have substantial effect on our international standing; if we were to pursue policies that forced some of the more important nations into a Soviet embrace, our global position could be critically undermined; or, if we were to respond ineffectually to a series of local challenges by Soviet proxies, our credibility and strength would suffer globally. In the new issues area, we find similar problems: Failure to gain support from India, Pakistan, Israel, South Africa, Brazil, and Argentina for nonproliferation objectives during the Carter administration meant not only that these countries were largely free to pursue their nuclear goals but that the cumulative effect of our failures made a global nonproliferation policy meaningless. Many critics of human-rights policies could make a similar point, but in those instances (and to some extent in the nonproliferation area) successes in individual countries and specific cases were worthwhile in themselves, even though they did not form a convincing pattern. Criticism should focus on whether regional policy failures harmed the related global policy and broader U.S. interests. Of course, moral policies have to be enunciated and pursued for normative reasons, even when they are not likely to be fully attained.[9]

If the United States is able to weigh and synthesize its global and regional concerns, it should have a more useful starting point for examining the possibilities for pursuing an effective policy in the Third World.

5.
THE CHOICE
OF STRATEGIES

Neither Isolation nor Hegemony

Within today's international setting, the United States can pursue several strategies in approaching the Third World, although some are more illusory than real. Briefly, the most salient strategies are

- A reassertion of U.S. leadership and global responsibility.
- An ad hoc policy of responding to events as they arise.
- An isolationist posture.
- A more or less explicit division of responsibility with the USSR.
- Continued U.S. involvement but at a much lower level.

The first of these strategies—a reassertion of earlier postwar patterns—is appealing and frequently finds its way into political rhetoric, if not actions. The past several years have seen a resurrection of this kind of thinking and even some actions taken in support of it. If anything stands out as the central message of this study, however, it is my conviction that a broad reassertion of U.S. primacy is not a feasible strategy for the long run or even in the midterm and that attempts in that direction will remain episodic at best. I will not belabor the point further here.

A large part of our Third World policy in the decades since World War II has been an ad hoc approach. Many times no general concepts were at work at all; at other times, either the economic or political concepts were set forth whereas the others were not; at still other times, several concepts directly competed with each other. There are worse approaches to policy than these ad hoc ones, especially when one is dealing with as diverse a group of nations as the Third World and when no broad national consensus defines what U.S. interests are there. Perhaps pursuing an approach involving no overall policy is less harmful than following a faulty one. We no longer, however, have the abundance of resources needed to permit such inexact policymaking.

An isolationist approach is equally a straw man, whether we follow it globally or selectively in our relations with the Third World countries, while continuing to interact with nations of the First and Second Worlds. The international system is too independent to permit pursuit of U.S. economic, political, or security interests without the inclusion of the Third World countries. Furthermore, maintaining at least the option of a global posture is inherent in the role of a superpower.

The United States is not Camelot. The death of John Kennedy and Richard Nixon's act of betrayal cannot be equated with Arthur and Lancelot. The castle still stands, the troops are fairly well armed, and a steady stream of suppliants for succor comes to the Oval Office, if not the Round Table. Even if the mythical past cannot be duplicated, the United States does have a global calling that it must pursue, even though this approach sometimes tests the limits of its capabilities. We have a unique global reach, and only a few places (Afghanistan is one) are outside our effective military power. Even though the United States no longer stands alone as the leading economic and military power, it is still the only nation at the forefront of both groupings. Even if we chose policies of isolation or rigid nonintervention, we would probably not be allowed to pursue them.[1]

Cooperation with the Soviet Union

A more cogent case can be made for cooperating with the Soviet Union in setting up spheres of influence or condominia for dealing with the Third World, thereby putting security responsibility squarely in the hands of those called upon and qualified to manage it—the two superpowers. (Economic management would presumably be based on a different system with parallel principles.) Moscow and Washington carry the burden of destructive capability, and they arguably owe it to themselves and the rest of the world to minimize the risk of their being drawn into a destructive war resulting from turmoil in the Third World. The Strategic Arms Limitation Talks (SALT) fell victim to events in Africa and Asia, and the pattern of conflicts since World War II suggests that a war could be triggered by competition for influence in the grey areas of the Third World.

There may be an even more compelling argument for the United States to cooperate with the Soviets. If we expect our relative position vis-à-vis the Soviets in the Third World to continue to decline in an approximately straight line, a codification of the present circumstances through a condominium would be in our interests. Moscow, for its part, would probably welcome a negotiated agreement that would provide the global equality that it so ardently pursues.

The argument for U.S.-Soviet accord, however, fails on several counts. First, the assumption that the Soviet Union is on the way to outstripping the United States is specious. Although during the early 1970s the Soviet Union claimed political and military parity worldwide, its ability to back up that claim varies greatly from region to region. U.S. distant operations capabilities in particular are far superior to those of the Soviet Union, and the U.S. military establishment has enjoyed a considerable renaissance in recent years. The Soviets may pull more or less even, for the impressive heritage of the Brezhnev buildup is in place, but parity is just that—it means that your opponent worries just as much as you do over the balance of forces. To call the worry a shift in the "correlation of forces"—thereby accepting the Soviet definition— does not change the actual situation.

The perceived shift in the Third World alignment since decolonization has been one of Western losses in areas previously, but no longer, controllable. That much is undeniable as long as one does not try to quantify too exactly what has been lost or to equate such losses with Soviet gains. In Iran, for example, we lost influence in and support of a nation that played a helpful role in stabilizing Southwest Asia. Opportunities for Soviet exploitation opened up, but, in the face of Iranian nationalism, the Soviets have not been able to further their interests there. Similarly, the Soviets are still seeking in India—one of their greatest success stories—in William Barnds' phrase, "the spoils that are supposed to go with victory."[2] New Delhi has conceded few points to the Soviets, and the flow of benefits in that relationship has been overwhelmingly southward. When the flow shows signs of reversing (as it has in the economic area) Indians show no reluctance to change the terms of the relationship to maintain their advantage. In Vietnam and Ethiopia, too, many chapters remain to be written.

U.S.-Soviet competition in the Third World will not be a zero-sum game unless the United States makes Stalin's mistake and forces it into that mold through rhetoric and actions. We are witnessing a trend toward multipolarity, a natural and inevitable devolution process in which new nations are asserting interests of independence and national development. For reasons discussed in Chapter 4, the Soviet Union is not terribly attractive to Third World countries, although some leadership groups may welcome the Leninist model of control. It is difficult to see how the Soviets will ever overcome their economic and cultural lag behind not just the United States but the entire Western world.

The Soviets have been most successful in military supply and security areas. Third World leaders have been impressed with Moscow's increased military capability, its readiness to supply arms to developing countries on attractive terms, and its fairly consistent policies. The ability to use force or to influence the terms of its use by others is a critical asset that the Soviets are willing to exploit when the opportunity arises. Yet Moscow does not set the conditions unilaterally. Individual Third World countries would put themselves in a position of subservience to Soviet policy only under the most extreme conditions, as the motley array of Soviet clients illustrates.

Condominium fails on other grounds as well. The United States and the Soviet Union have been moving away from cooperation across the whole range of their relations, and the contest of influence in the Third World lies at the root of this sharpened rivalry. Even at the high point of détente in 1972, the Moscow Agreement offered only dangerously vague language about relations between the two superpowers in the Third World. Neither power trusts the other for good reason. The temptation to poach would be immense on each side if opportunities were to arise in the camp of the other. Nothing in Soviet history or ideology suggests that its drive would stop with achievement of parity, even if Moscow has no specific plans at this time. Poaching has been generally avoided in Europe because the lines are clearly drawn, the problem is of fairly narrow compass, and the danger of retribution certain and awful. It would be impossible to approach the far-flung Third World with similar rigor, and the problems that arose in settling on the European dividing line in the late 1940s are warning enough not to try to duplicate the process under current conditions.

Condominium would almost certainly be rejected by U.S. public opinion. It would require high levels of coordinated U.S. and Soviet pressure—frequently violent—to force today's Third World nations into such a structure. Third World nations are responsible for working out their own destinies, even if they involve rather unpleasant means. As long as the overall international order or vital interests of the superpowers are not in clear and present danger, it is neither proper nor useful for them to become involved. The United States and the Soviet Union are not responsible for everything that goes on in the world, and, as our experiences demonstrate, the United States is not very successful when it plays the global role of policeman or social worker. U.S. interests would be best devoted to ensuring that the Soviets do not intervene unilaterally in the painful process as the new nations work out their troubled destinies.

Rejecting the strategy of condominium does not determine the role that the Soviet Union should play in the Third World. An exclusion approach is even more unrealistic than one based on condominium. Let us return to the idea of the Soviet Union as a claimant for a larger share of the international power and influence pie and as a nation whose claim is credible, if unwelcome. The alternative to acceding to that claim is to contest it forcefully: That has been a major theme of U.S. policy since the late 1940s. The vehemence with which we have contested has varied greatly, ranging from armed force to attempts to preempt the economic and military assistance possibilities in certain countries.

During the Nixon and Carter administrations, more sophisticated strategies of dealing with the Soviets were devised. The United States saw the Moscow Basic Principles Agreement of 1972 which forswore attempts by either party to gain unilateral advantage at the expense of the other, as putting the Third World off limits to competition, and the early Carter administration exuded a global optimism based on the assumption that the Soviets were well on the way to losing the contest for influence in the Third World. Although neither strategy turned out to be very effective, each rested on a substantial premise. If the Soviet Union could either be excluded from Third World competition through a self-denying ordinance or if the context of the game could be kept in nonmilitary forms, either or both strategies could have been brilliant successes; as we have seen, the Soviet Union is hardly competitive in nonsecurity areas. Unfortunately, this fact is not lost on the Soviets.

It is questionable whether Moscow took the 1972 agreement very seriously, and, even if it did, it did so in terms incompatible with U.S. assumptions. For exercising restraint in the Third World, the Soviets would have expected a voice in regional matters commensurate with their estimate of their own importance. Certainly the examples from history were not encouraging: One need not be a revisionist historian to see that Truman and even Roosevelt engaged in sharp practices designed to minimize Soviet positions in Eastern Europe; nor need one be a strident liberationist to see that Stalin acted in abominably bad faith. In the Congo operations of 1960, U.S. policy systematically denied the Soviets the role it would readily have granted to another power of equal capabilities and pretensions. Yet what sensible U.S. leader could have trusted Khrushchev to play a responsible role?

After the 1972 agreement, the issue of U.S.-Soviet competition took shape most clearly in the Middle East crisis of 1973. No matter how one interprets U.S. and Soviet behavior, the results showed the emptiness of the agreement. On one hand, the Soviets must be faulted for their irresponsibility before the outbreak of hostilities and especially in the early course of the fighting. Moscow blatantly maneuvered to gain unilateral advantage from the situation. On the other hand, by uncompromisingly excluding the Soviets from having a voice after the crisis, the United States demonstrated that it would not yield place to the Soviets ex gratia and that Kissinger's views of the need to bring the Soviet Union more fully into the international system would remain theoretical.[3]

By "declaring victory" in the Third World, the Carter administration made explicit a situation that the Soviets could not tolerate. Despite an aborted attempt to give the Soviets some standing in the Middle East, minimizing Soviet embarrassment over their ouster from Somalia, and exemplary restraint in not exploiting the potential advantage in the Zaire unrest of 1977, Washington was not able to consolidate a status quo that was highly unfavorable to Soviet aspirations.[4] The Soviets had already demonstrated in Angola that they would not forego their military trump cards, and the extension of indirect intervention into Ethiopia and Kampuchea fatally undermined U.S. hopes of confining the competition to those aspects in which it held the high cards. Although the Soviet invasion of Afghanistan was arguably an event of a different nature since it was a response to a perceived direct security threat, it put the final nail in the coffin of accord. The two superpowers were left with no basis for mutual restraint or cooperation; the United States was left without a viable policy concept beyond reflexive globalism. This situation persisted for several years.

Obviously such a situation is dangerously unsatisfactory, but it is difficult to find ways of doing something about it. Given the power and ambitions of the Soviets, it is unthinkable that they will be permanently excluded from an important voice in Middle East affairs. They have allies there, they have opportunities to exploit tensions through various forms of security assistance, and the area is undeniably of as great geostrategic importance to them as it is to us. By courting Vietnam, Moscow has been able to secure a foothold in Southeast Asia, and, in the longer term, a substantial Soviet role is attractive to several of the ASEAN nations who see China as a greater threat. In South Asia the Soviets already have the strongest outside voice. Africa and Latin America are much further afield, but growing Soviet capabilities, plus the universal structure of global politics, suggest that it will be difficult to completely exclude them from these regions. As long as there are uncontained disputes within Third World regions or countries that feel themselves exposed to intolerable threats, some nations will anxiously look to one of the superpowers for geopolitical and security assistance.

For at least the foreseeable future, the United States and the Soviet Union are going to have to deal with each other on the basis of power realities, without any illusions like those generated by détente in the

1970s and with appropriately modest objectives. This situation will not be easy for the United States to live with. Lacking broad-spectrum capabilities, Moscow will approach the Third World on a piecemeal basis, looking for openings to lend security support and supply arms. Not only is this their strong suit; it also plays directly against our weakness—reluctance to use military force—and leaves the choice of terrain largely to them. We could find ourselves challenged at almost any location and forced to defend a status quo as unattractive as whatever alternative the Soviets support.

In the past the United States has been able to take a fairly relaxed view of Soviet gains in the Third World. Local governments had a demonstrated ability to reverse those gains when they tired of Soviet involvement. We can no longer be quite so relaxed. Although local regimes still can evict the Soviets or their proxies in most cases, they may find it increasingly difficult as Moscow develops its capability to move troops and equipment over long distances. Some faction will always assess that its own advantage is served by maintaining a Soviet tie. If the faction is strong enough to put up a struggle and hold on for a while, the Soviets could consider assisting it as the legitimate bearer of the people's will. A long-distance Brezhnev Doctrine should not be in the cards as long as we can maintain deterrent air and naval capabilities and are willing to interpose them; we may, however, find ourselves faced with dangerous situations that could not previously have arisen.

One disturbing trend is the increase in the Soviet efforts to entrench their supporters and to work for the establishment of reasonably serious, Marxist-Leninist cadre parties in friendly countries. Their efforts in Ethiopia, for example, are destined to ensure that should Colonel Mengistu tire of the Soviet presence, he will be much more constrained from ousting them than was Anwar Sadat in Egypt. Another type of development could be equally serious. Should the Soviets succeed in gaining influence over friendly regimes in two neighboring countries, they could bring the advantages of geographic contiguity into play, as they have in Eastern Europe and Afghanistan. Pro-Soviet elements under pressure in one country may call upon their colleagues in the other for support, and the United States might be in no position to interdict it. Although such situations do not exist now, the potential was there briefly in the Horn of Africa (Somalia and Ethiopia); likewise, it can be seen today in Libya, which borders on several vulnerable countries, and should a Communist regime in El Salvador join one in Nicaragua, they could be mutually supportive. This sort of situation may be where the domino theory has meaning, and the United States would do well to direct some attention to places where this sort of Soviet regionalism is a real possibility.

Although the United States has no wholly satisfactory strategy for meeting the Soviet Third World challenge, important partial strategies are available. By maintaining strong, highly mobile military capabilities, the United States can shift the decision to escalate conflicts to the Soviets. By maintaining our economic and political advantages, we should be able to asert our interests in almost all (but, unfortunately, not quite all) situations. The poor overall state of U.S.-Soviet relations does not absolve us from seeking to reduce the danger to our relationship that stems from Third World issues—especially since those issues were so instrumental in bringing about the current situation—and from ameliorating the competition, even if only marginally. In its simplest form this approach would mean developing a better understanding of what each side is likely to do in the Third World. Although no country is going to give away its innermost state secrets, the United States could benefit from meeting with the Soviets to discuss policy toward the Third World nations; periodic political exchange could reduce unpredictability and avoid unnecessary confrontations. The level of these meetings should not be high; our assistant secretaries of state, or, perhaps more preferable, personnel still further down the working levels should be involved. By keeping discussions routine and inconspicuous, we can sidestep the dilemma that high-level contacts are a political act in themselves so cannot be held in times of brewing crisis—of course the time when communications are most needed. A good start of this approach was the series of subcabinet-level meetings in 1984 and 1985. The first of these was a meeting on the Iran-Iraq War, a situation with high potential for U.S.-Soviet involvement. Subsequent meetings on the Far and Middle East, Africa and Central America have been more routine and apparently have involved only exchanges of concerns and views. At the present stage of U.S.-Soviet relations, these constitute an appropriate beginning for a process of ongoing consultation.

Through such contacts we could explore the possible mutually acceptable rules of the game, such as agreement to prevent each super-power's allies or clients from engaging in activities on their own account that are inimical to the global system. (It is too much to expect that the superpowers would forego the use of proxies for their own benefit.) Some system of incentives and sanctions should be developed to en-courage Third World powers to support aspects of the global system (such as a nonproliferation regime) in the mutual interest of the super-powers. Frankly, it is difficult to see many possibilities beyond these, especially regarding such matters as limitations of arms sales, that would put direct restraints on the superpowers. Nevertheless, the United States could look for partial steps for socializing the Soviet Union, an area in which little effort is being expended here or in Moscow.

The task, however, is not completely hopeless. Soviet officials say that they are being increasingly cautious in dealing with the Third World now that they have a greater positive stake there.[5] Although this may be disinformation, there is no doubt that up to 1979 the Soviet Union exerted a more stabilizing force in South Asia (where it has been heavily committed for nearly a generation) than in other areas where its responsibilities were less important. In an area in which it enjoys a role that is satisfactory by its own standards, the Soviet Union would be interested in being on good terms with as many regional states as possible, rather than choosing sides and fomenting dissention. (The extreme case is Eastern Europe.) Without a satisfactory stake in the region, the Soviets would perhaps see their interest best served by unrest and would attempt to promote it. Although we may not find many regional situations "satisfactory" to both us and the Soviets, we should keep looking. Putting the situation in these terms refocuses U.S. attention where it can be more profitably applied—not on the U.S.-Soviet bilateral relationship but on those parts of the world in which most unrest takes place.

Devolution of Responsibility

The final policy approach for the United States would be to make every effort to encourage Third World countries and subsystems to assume resonsibility for their own security with minimum U.S. involvement—and that at a distance. This strategy would be consistent with the principle of subsidiarity by which responsibilities should rest at the lowest competent level. The United States would, of course, reserve the right to act unilaterally to protect its own vital interests when they were seriously threatened and regional forces were unable or unwilling to protect them adequately.

Much of our recent international involvement can be seen as a pull and tug between the perceptions of global responsibility on the one hand and a preference for devolution on the other; thus, we have a considerable body of historical evidence that should give us some idea of what devolution entails. Even the Truman Doctrine was offered to the public as a means of helping others take care of themselves, as indeed it was. Under the Truman Doctrine, however, and still more in the 1950s, the U.S. share of joint security responsibility was by far the larger. Join security arrangements involved little more than alliances in which the United States provided leadership and resources while other members were committed only to help defend themselves if necessary.

This approach was reasonable in an era of abundant resources and overwhelming U.S. superiority, but during the 1960s, it was subjected to a radical rethinking as U.S. resources declined, Vietnam sapped the nation's will, and the capabilities of some Third World states began to grow.

The so-called Nixon Doctrine marked a dramatic revision in U.S. views of its role in the world, much as the downgrading of the dollar's role was to do a few years later in international finance. Like the economic shift, however, the Nixon Doctrine did not come fully to terms with the underlying realities. The United States hesitated to adjust its role downward as far as the circumstances demanded, and the rest of the world was unprepared for a drastic decline in U.S. responsibilities. However, coming at a time of change that was rapid but not completely clear in its direction, the Nixon Doctrine was an important step. Its assumption that others should bear the main burden for their defense was a sound one, which we had too long failed to grasp. We often acted, as Henry Kissinger observed, as if others' security were more important to us than to them. Nixon also rightly perceived that the United States would have to continue to provide an overall security structure by maintaining the global balance vis-à-vis the Soviet Union.

Despite notable success in the Gulf region and passable grades in the impossible situation in Vietnam, the doctrine was flawed by a basic, if only implicit, conceptual error. In the relentlessly global view of Nixon and Kissinger, Third World countries continued to be objects in the international order, with limited capacity for useful, independent action. The word *proxies* was often used to describe the role allocated to countries such as Iran or Thailand, implying that such allies would act in the place or on behalf of the United States. U.S. policies and priorities would define the proxy's actions, for the East-West competition was of such overriding importance—and only we, as a superpower, knew how to handle it—that the priorities and preferences of other nations would have to be subordinate to it. To be sure, our clients were to be rewarded (with nuclear umbrella, arms supply, and economic assistance), and they would in theory be able to pursue their own subglobal interests. The United States remained closely identified with the domestic and regional policies of its proxies and acquired some responsibility for their excesses and failures.

If a nation is going to accept proxy status, it must be either very scared or very desperate for resources. As the Soviets are now discovering, nations meeting these criteria are not numerous and those that do qualify probably will not contribute much to the common endeavor. Even the glowing success of the Nixon Doctrine came about not because Iran was willing to act as a U.S. proxy but because the shah saw his security interests in terms parallel to our own. His actions on the oil price front were not those of a proxy, and they may even have harmed our overall security interests more than Iran had helped them elsewhere. Therefore, although the Nixon Doctrine was an improtant step, it failed to deal with emerging regional relations and is not a useful model for our future behavior.

Trends toward greater autonomy and capability in the Third World were still inchoate in the Nixon years; during the 1970s the new strength and importance of the periphery became manifest. The 1973 oil crisis and the moves to create a bargaining front in the South against the affluent North were important economic elements. These were reinforced by substantial military buildups in a number of Third World states and by initial steps toward greater regional cooperation, all set against a background of apparent decline in both U.S. and Soviet assertiveness in Third World matters. Kissinger had begun to draw appropriate conclusions from this changing situation, and the Carter administration sought to develop the implications of devolution in support of U.S. interests. Of the ten foreign-policy goals that Zbigniew Brzezinski proposed to the president at the beginning of the Carter administration, half were concerned with North-South affairs; only two were devoted to U.S.-Soviet relations.[6] The objectives were impressive: to take greater account of the aspirations of Third World nations; to redefine issues in North-South, rather than East-West, terms; and, to develop policies responsive to Third World needs. This new approach seemed to correct the basic weakness of the Nixon Doctrine by treating Third World nations as subjects of international politics rather than as mere objects and by recognizing that our role would involve less direction than acceptance of common goals. The underlying rationale of the policy was that Third World nations, with their new strength, would be the arbiters of whether or not Moscow would be able to play its military trump cards and that the inherent strength and attractiveness of the West, underpinned by sound U.S. policy, guaranteed a favorable outcome.

After two or three years, this brave new approach was in shambles. Part of the problem was bad luck (the fall of the shah and of Daud Kahn in Afghanistan), and part was the inability of the U.S. public to recognize the value of such positive moves as the Panama Canal Treaty and increased economic assistance programs. There was also an exaggerated assumption by the U.S. government that some important regimes in the Third World would become virtual allies of the United States—an expectation that was hardly more realistic than the hopes during the Nixon period of recruiting proxies. When these expectations were not met, disappointment turned to bitterness, for example, with India and Argentina following the Soviet invasion of Afghanistan. The main problem, however, was the United States' underestimation of remaining Soviet potential for mischief making in the Third World and its weak nerves in allowing problems to work themselves out. Although Carter and Brzezinski had developed an impressive policy design, the president's political weaknesses and the divided counsels within the administration probably made it impossible to carry out, even with less Soviet pressure. In the last part of Carter's term, attention rapidly shifted away from the earlier North-South strategy and toward renewed preoccupation with the Soviet danger—a line that the Reagan administration elevated to a key element of its foreign policy.[7]

Throughout Reagan's first term, there was no clear policy line toward the Third World, but during 1985, a Reagan Doctrine began to make its appearance. It involved support to insurgent groups who are fighting against Soviet-supported regimes in such diverse places as Nicaragua, Angola, Afghanistan, and Kampuchea. It reflected a determination not to yield the initiative in the Third World to Moscow, the charge that had been leveled against the Carter administration in the late 1970s as the Soviets profited from a series of opportunities in Africa, Asia, and Central Ameria. This new approach was put into a larger context in a presidential message to the Congress of March 14, 1986—the long overdue codification of the Reagan administration's Third World policy. Although it focused heavily on support for insurgent forces opposing Marxist regimes, it also noted the need for such mundane things as improved trading opportunities for Third World exporters and enunciated clearly the proposition that most Third World problems were indigenous and not the result of Soviet machinations. For the Reagan administration, this was a considerable intellectual concession.

It is not yet clear whether the broader context of the March 14 message was merely sugarcoating to win support for anti-Marxist "freedom fighters" or whether it represents a more seasoned view of the realities of the Third World. It does, however, provide the framework for a more fruitful policy than has been available for the first half of the 1980s.

In any event, the Reagan policies are reminiscent of the roll-back philosophy in vogue in the 1950s and go beyond merely helping insurgents. Strenuous attempts to woo India through economic and military sales incentives, in place now for over two years, reflect an equal determination to contest against the Soviets in areas in which they are perceived to have made significant political headway.

If the Reagan approach is pursued single-mindedly as a part of the U.S.-Soviet competition, it is likely to lead to another disaster of U.S. globalism. If, however, the tender shoots of regionalism apparent in the March 14 statement are allowed to flourish, the United States could be approaching a sensible Third World policy. The Soviet Union cannot be given a free hand, and adjustments to the policies of the early Carter years were needed as the global situation changed. A sober case-by-case analysis would no doubt indicate where a more combative position is in order when dealing with the Soviet Union and its clients and would show that the United States has to make some effort in countries like India if it is not to leave the field to Moscow.

The setbacks to Brzezinski's policy of global optimism do not invalidate the assumptions on which it is based, and an overzealous implementation of the Reagan Doctrine could lose a promising baby in the change of bathwater. In the 1980s, the United States can no longer define its role in the Third World principally in terms of its relations with the Soviet Union; nor is it the sole guarantor of a decent international order. We should use the devolution of power to our advantage, rather than risking our substance in a futile battle against it. Until regional autonomy is developed to the point that the Ethiopias of this world see more benefit in preserving autonomy than in calling for superpower intervention, there will be need for attractive policies, for a realistic appraisal of regional strengths, and certainly for a means to deal with Soviet assertiveness.

The responsibilities for the Third World can devolve in various ways, and some will go to our European and Japanese allies. They have new capabilities and should bear their share of the global burden. Several of our allies have begun to play helpful economic roles in the Third World, and France has undertaken a direct security role, especially in the nations of francophone Africa. Desirable as this activity may be, it falls far short of meeting the overall security problems facing the United States, its allies, and those nations of the Third World who wish to maintain a nonaligned or even pro-Western policy. As we look to the future, the bulk of the responsibility must devolve to the developing countries themselves. They are familiar with the issues; their interests are most critically at stake; and they are gaining relative strength in the shift of global power that has been taking place since the end of World War II.

6.
THE SITUATION
IN INDIVIDUAL REGIONS

I HAVE USED MOSTLY ABSTRACTIONS and generalizations in discussing U.S. strategies and the regional subsystems and their relationship to the global system. To return to the real world, we need to take a close look at several parts of the Third World to see how U.S. policy affects them. Voluminous literature has been published on all of these regions,[1] and it would be pointless to replicate even a small part of it here. In the following pages I shall attempt to point out some specifics of recent history and current situations that are especially important for understanding the particular issues that form the core of this study. These specifics should provide a partial framework within which the reader can consider policy preferences for individual regions and, especially, for a general approach toward the Third World. The regions I will describe are Southeast Asia, the South Asian subcontinent, the Gulf area, Southern Africa, and Central America. For the last three regions I have sought to provide a broader setting, although both Africa and Latin America are too unwieldy to serve as useful analytical frameworks. I treat the Middle East at greater length—not to provide a comprehensive analysis but rather to illustrate the problems of a system overloaded with internal dissentions and external pressures.

Southeast Asia

The starting point for any discussion of regional security maintenance in the Third World must be Southeast Asia.[2] If Southeast Asia and ASEAN did not exist, authors would have to invent them to illustrate the kinds of opportunities and problems that arise when a group of nations, subjected to the severest external buffeting, undertake to organize for some degree of protection. We must not, of course, assume that Southeast Asia and its regional institutions are the model for the Third World. However, its institutions function better and show more promise than do those of any other region, so that it is a useful starting point.

Southeast Asia is much farther along a (not *the*) road of regional development for very good reasons. The region, like Europe, has learned the hard way what it means to lie on a fault line of the global political structure. It has been the arena for contests, sometimes bitter ones, between the United States and some combination (or succession) of China, the Soviet Union, and local Communists. In such situations, simple survival demands a high level of skill in international maneuvering. In addition, the nations of Southeast Asia have been much more successful economically than have most other Third World states, and, whether as individual nations or as a grouping, Southeast Asia has benefited from some farsighted and talented leaders who exhibited uncommon pragmatism.

The emergence of a Southeast Asian system in its present configuration was not a foregone conclusion. The region is ethnically diverse, contains nations of vastly different size and economic development, and has no particular historical justification. It is little more than what is left after one has subtracted China and India. The principal unifying security factor in the system is concern about China, and even this concern is shared unevenly among members. System boundaries are not determined by any compelling logic; Vietnam, though certainly part of Southeast Asia, stands resolutely aside from the mainstream, as has Burma. Outside observers—both political scientists and U.S. presidents—have frequently thought that a tidier arrangement would include India, which could lead a southern Asian system.

Southeast Asia has been rent by internal disputes, not only between Communist and non-Communist components but among the latter group. Both Indonesia and the Philippines sought to undermine the integrity of Malaysia, and Indonesia did not hesitate to use force. Substantial bitterness also developed between Singapore and Malaysia, and several local insurgencies stretched across the internal borders of the ASEAN countries. For a small group of states, this menu of conflict was fairly extensive, but no matter in dispute was either so important or so bitterly contested that it made cooperation impossible.

The Southeast Asian subsystem also had to face the problem of Indonesia—a member much larger than the others and a candidate to become a global middle power or regional influential. Even more difficult, Indonesia under President Sukarno was one of the looser cannons on the international decks and posed a severe security problem for its neighbors; under Sukarno's leadership, there was no prospect for effective cooperation among the states of Southeast Asia nor was any grouping viable that excluded Indonesia.

The problem of Vietnam is especially difficult. Hanoi, by virtue of its expansionist activities and ideological commitment, presents the classic threat of a nation that is both an outsider and a potential member to a Southeast Asian regional security system. As long as the Vietnamese economic and political systems are so different from those of the other regional states, it is hard to see how lasting cooperation would be possible. On the other hand, none of the disputes between Vietnam and its Southeast Asian neighbors is so serious that it cannot be solved.

In the short term, the main problem presented by Vietnam is its relationship to outside forces, notably the Soviet Union. Such externalities have been a lasting feature of the Southeast Asian scene. Hanoi was always dependent on substantial Soviet and Chinese support, Britain had defense arrangements with Malaysia and Singapore, the United States traditionally had a close relationship with the Philippines, and the Southeast Asia Treaty Organization (SEATO) pact drew in still other external powers. Although pulls came from many different directions, none had a great degree of staying power. Britain left the region as part of its withdrawal from east of the Suez in the late 1960s; the United States seemed to exhaust its interest after defeat in Vietnam; the Chinese broke with Vietnam; and Pakistan and France fell by the wayside. The Soviet link to Hanoi has yet to be tested.

All these challenges contributed to the emergence of cooperation in Southeast Asia. Sukarno's regional misbehavior contributed to his ouster and provided an object lesson for his successors: Indonesia could ultimately play a stronger international role if it enjoyed regional support, and in the short run the country would be best served by concentrating on domestic rebuilding. Indonesia had been socialized into regional cooperation, and in the process it had provided a strong but not domineering core around which its neighbors could rally. External alliance systems also ultimately contributed to regional rapprochement. The collapse of Sukarno's dream of Afro-Asian leadership pointed Indonesia still further inward; British withdrawal forced its former colonies to look for alternatives; U.S. disengagement cautioned all regional states that they could no longer comfortably assume that a protective umbrella would be available indefinitely.

Another factor of major importance to regional cooperation was the emergence of an external threat, Vietnam, a potential member of the subsystem. A unified Vietnam that had shown its mettle against the United States was threatening enough. Once Hanoi made common cause with Moscow, however, and demonstrated through its invasion of Kampuchea that it had ambition beyond its own borders, the other states of Southeast Asia had an additional incentive to arrange for their individual and regional security. In sum, in less than a generation Southeast Asia had undergone a wide variety of experiences well designed to show that the outside world was a dangerous place and that a substantial part of the region's survival depended upon the subsystem itself. This realization must be transformed into purposeful activity, and even then sufficient strength may not be available to ensure survival.

Southeast Asia had already made some steps that could be called purposeful activities: Several organizations in the 1950s and 1960s were either regionwide or embraced several members, and the SEATO and U.K.-sponsored Five Power Defense pacts and some pan-Asian groupings brought several regional nations into contact with each other. A basis for economic cooperation had begun to develop in response to the nations' common involvement with Japan and the United States, and all regional states shared a preference for private economic development.

During the ten years between Sukarno's fall and U.S. withdrawal from Vietnam, the Southeast Asian states began a process of organization through ASEAN, founded in 1967. The group's beginnings were extremely modest. Through past experience the states had learned to expect progress only in small steps, and for some years ASEAN was hardly an organization at all. It lacked a secretariat until 1974; it held no summit until 1976; the organization was too fragile to attempt to resolve disputes among its members; and, even in the economic sphere, the potential for cooperation was very limited—less a matter of coordinating the members' internal economies than of developing techniques for a common approach to the outside world. Decisions were made by consensus, and great care was taken not to alienate any member. Underlying the whole operation, however, were the realizations that (1) Southeast Asia needed to find both political and economic ways of dealing with intrusive great powers on terms that reflected Southeast Asian needs rather than the imposition of others' requirements and (2) that cooperation was worth the price of toning down intraregional disputes.

Although external events focused the attention of ASEAN members, the more likely threats to their security were not armed attack by Vietnam, the Soviet Union, or China but those arising from their own internal weaknesses. Despite their economic development and political stability, these were new nations, and they shared the general problems of developing countries. Indonesia preached the need for Southeast Asian resilience—a combination of economic development, strong government, and military capability sufficient to deter external attack and to demonstrate that the region deserved support. Among these elements, military capability was less important than internal security cooperation among

ASEAN members in dealing with insurgencies and subversive threats because no outside help could be expected to do much good.

The very slow process of development of ASEAN worked well: By moving one step at a time, the organization avoided mistakes and did not overload its circuits. By the late 1970s, it had become a recognized international actor, and, though the political and economic conditions of its members were hardly resilient, impressive progress had resulted. If the United States had made its sacrifice in Vietnam to some extent to protect the rest of Southeast Asia, the beneficiaries of U.S. policy had used the time well. If these nations had once been dominoes, they now had fairly stable foundations.

ASEAN had two broad options for dealing with the outside world: It could attempt to exclude all foreign power involvement or it could promote a balance of countervailing external influences in the region. Either option would produce the same net effect—providing maximum freedom to maneuver. Members were divided about the choice of options, and, after the end of the Vietnam war, opinion swung toward exclusion, since the Soviets were already at a distance, the Americans moving off, and the Chinese restrained. A proposal for a Zone of Peace, Freedom and Neutrality (ZOPFAN) was adopted in 1971 as ASEAN's long-term goal, and for the next several years its sponsors cultivated it on the grounds that growing strength of ASEAN members and the continuing U.S. withdrawal provided the opportunity and the need for assertion of a semi-armed neutrality status. Inherent in the ZOPFAN concept was the belief that Vietnam would be gradually attracted into it; otherwise, superior Vietnamese military capabilities would pose a constant threat to its members. Vietnam seemed like a prospective member; once the United States had departed, sponsors assumed that Hanoi would want to rebuild its economy and society and avoid excessive dependence on its erstwhile Soviet or Chinese patrons.

The mid-1970s was a high point for potential Southeast Asian autonomy, and after years of slow progress, the formal structure began to take on a more authoritative shape. ASEAN leaders held their first summit in 1976, and two years later ASEAN emerged as an international actor, as role underlined by cabinet-level contacts among ASEAN, the United States, and the European Community (EC). In the following years, the U.S. secretary of state and representatives from Canada, Japan, Australia, the United Kingdom, and New Zealand attended the annual ministerial meeting. In 1978, ASEAN began formal dealings with its European counterpart, the EC. Even the broader international environment was propitious. By the mid-1970s détente was in full flower; Sino-American rapprochement had begun and the Sino-Soviet dispute seemed distant. If the United States and the Soviet Union were sincere about foregoing unilateral advantages in the Third World, Southeast Asia would have been a fine place to demonstrate it, for neither side perceived its security interests there as very high.

During the last two years of the decade, the context changed profoundly. On the global scene, détente turned into bitter recriminations and sanctions. Furthermore, China normalized its relations with the United States and reached a treaty agreement with Japan that further solidified a new power arrangement in Asia—the United States, China, and Japan loosely but effectively associated against Soviet expansionism. The United States concluded that it would have to play a larger role in Asian affairs than it had anticipated at the end of the Vietnam war. Since it had failed to repair relations with Hanoi, U.S. reinvolvement was going to have to be in association with ASEAN.

Events within Southeast Asia contributed to more active participations of the great powers in the region. Vietnam found itself at odds with the Pol Pot regime in Kampuchea and faced with domestic difficulties. Hanoi responded by invading Kampuchea and by expelling its own ethnic Chinese; both of these actions had profound effects on ASEAN and beyond its sphere. By invading Kampuchea Vietnam showed that it would not accommodate itself to its regional environment, and it had turned decisively toward the Soviets to gain the political and economic backing for the Kampuchean adventure. This move fully alienated China and introduced the Soviet Union into the workings of the Southeast Asian system to a much greater extent than ever before. Southeast Asia had once again become the cockpit of great-power rivalry, but this time the opponents were the Soviet Union and China, with the United States standing somewhat to the side.

Problems for the region were further compounded by the flood of Chinese refugees; by the continuing resistance to the Vietnamese invasion by Pol Pot forces along the Thai border, which threatened direct conflict between Vietnam and an ASEAN member; and by the Soviets' new access to bases in southern Vietnam. As ZOPFAN receded into a hazy, distant future, ASEAN had to look to its other option—the establishment of a power balance among outside forces. At the same time, individual ASEAN nations began to examine their own military preparedness and to intensify military cooperation among themselves on bilateral and multilateral bases. Thailand, in particular, was now on the front line and became the object of solicitous attention, tempered with concern that ties between Bangkok and Beijing not become overly close.

ASEAN's political responses have been impressive. It has taken the initiative in organizing international opinion on the Kampuchean question. Through a firm unity that masks some serious, internal differences of opinion, ASEAN has ensured that international opinion has continued to focus on the Vietnamese invasion of Kampuchea. Because a determined set of neighbors are in the vanguard, it is difficult for the Soviets and Vietnamese to pass off global criticism as cold-war rhetoric as they could if the United States had led the crusade. ASEAN has not brought about an acceptable end to the conflict, nor has it been able to set the terms of Chinese (much less Soviet) involvement, but ASEAN has emerged as a respected international actor whereas much of Vietnam's aura of virtue has washed away. In the new regional power configuration, Vietnam, not the nations previously regarded as Western puppets, has had to seek outside support to maintain itself and its legitimacy.

At the same time, ASEAN has shown considerable skill in orchestrating the balance-of-power relationships in the region. It has turned to the United States not as a weak suitor but as an international peer with considerable freedom of action, and Washington has recognized that it must shape its policies on such issues as aid to the Kampuchean resistance in concert with ASEAN. Even Hanoi and Moscow, though obviously unhappy with ASEAN, have found it advisable to mute their hostility and court, rather than coerce, the organization and its members.

This picture of the situation in Southeast Asia and in ASEAN is admittedly very rosy; very little would be required for the entire structure to collapse. The United States, the Soviet Union, and China could each take actions that would make ASEAN irrelevant, whereas economic developments in Japan, as well as in the United States, could wreck ASEAN's much-prized resilience. Old problems among the member states could resurface, and the accord on policy toward Kampuchea masks potentially damaging differences of view. Yet it is extremely important for the United States in particular to focus on what has been and could be accomplished. Former clients and putative dominoes have taken significant steps toward managing their regional security environment after the United States made considerable shambles of the neighborhood. If we could freeze the present situation in time, U.S. interests would be admirably served. As we look to the future of Southeast Asia, we would do well to focus on these positive developments—not unrealistically but with sober concern for how we can best align ourselves with them.

U.S. interests in the ASEAN region are substantial and fairly direct. ASEAN as a group is now our fourth largest trading partner, and it generally plays a singularly constructive role in North-South discussions and the international economic arena. Our investments there are significant, and several important raw materials come to us or our allies from the countries of ASEAN. Existing trade problems will probably grow as protectionist pressures develop, but economic differences have been handled pragmatically. Other U.S. priorities and interests in the areas of economics and global issues generally raise few problems. Complicated questions concerning refugees from Indochina are being handled smoothly. Serious differences concerning right of passage by U.S. warships through Indonesian territorial waters (an issue over which Indonesia's position conflicted with U.S. global freedom of navigation policies) are less irritating than they were a few years ago. Human rights violations continue to be present in several Southeast Asian countries aside from Indochina, for those who are inclined to look for them. The most difficult and obtrusive human rights problem has been removed for the time being at least by the departure of the Marcos regime from the Philippines.

The removal of Marcos does not, however, do much to change the other pressing issue of U.S.-Philippine relations, the status of our military facilities there and the economic assistance that Manila extracts in payment. The conditions of the Marcos-Aquino transition have, however, forced us to take a closer look at the question of the bases and their role in our global and regional strategy.

The purpose of the U.S. bases is an important issue to the United States, the Philippines, and ASEAN. The bases cannot be justified as necessary for defense of the Philippines as such, since nobody is likely to attack the islands. Our principal reason for maintaining them does not even relate to Southeast Asia, for few threats to which our friends there are exposed can be dealt with by U.S. armed force. Clark Field and Subic Bay are important as part of a global system of air and naval bases and as a key to our position in the southwest Pacific, the Indian Ocean, and the Gulf. Because facilities in Vietnam are under Soviet control, the Philippine bases take on still greater importance. The Philippine government is fully aware of this situation, and our global priorities sharply limit our negotiating flexibility.

We also have to view the bases from ASEAN's perspective. Since the Soviets are in Vietnam and since ASEAN strategy is based on a balance of external forces, it is in ASEAN's interests that the United States maintain its involvement. Clark and Subic bases are the most prominent symbols of our presence. If anybody took seriously Marcos's July 1983 threat to seek Soviet help if the United States did not meet his rent demands for Clark and Subic, concern should have been much greater in the other ASEAN capitals (and in Tokyo) than in Washington. ASEAN's security policies thus help the United States maintain the kind of position that it wants in Southeast Asia, and they will continue to do so as long as we are useful in regional concerns and as the Philippine bases are seen as an expression of U.S. global capability, not simply as an adjunct of U.S. global concerns. If ASEAN countries are ever able to bring ZOPFAN into existence, the Philippine bases would become a bargaining chip for ASEAN to play against removal of Soviet presence in Vietnam. This approach would result in an excruciating conflict of interest for the United States since, from its viewpoint, much of the broader mission of U.S. bases would remain even if the Soviets left Cam Ranh Bay.

The problem of the Philippine bases will not be solved in the short term. The Soviet threat to ASEAN is negligible and fairly distant because of countervailing U.S. capability. The problem of Vietnam is more pressing, but, aside from arms sales, the United States cannot do much about it militarily, and in any event the ASEAN countries prefer to handle the issue through diplomacy. In the middle range of threat stands China, nearer than the Soviet Union but for the while at least sharing ASEAN's interests of containing Vietnam and providing direct support to Thailand. However, Chinese and ASEAN midterm intentions differ considerably regarding Vietnam, and these differences are relevant to U.S. policy. Beijing seeks to ultimately establish some degree of ascendancy over Hanoi and to force it to abandon its alignment with Moscow. In any case, Vietnam will remain an actual or potential discordant element in Southeast Asia, some kind of cold-war fault line will continue to run through the area, and great-power involvement will persist. ASEAN, on the other hand, sees its interests as better served by reaching out to Vietnam and building it into a Southeast Asian system once the Kampuchean problem is out of the way. The establishment of ZOPFAN remains a goal, if a postponed one.

The United States must make some important choices regarding ASEAN. For reasons of global politics (related mainly to U.S. desire to maintain a common front with China against the Soviet Union), it might be in our interest to follow Beijing's lead in polarizing the situation in Indochina, keeping pressure on Vietnam and the Soviet Union, and working to build ASEAN still further into a strategic consensus that would include the United States, China, and Japan. Undoubtedly, the Soviets see Southeast Asia in global terms, and we may have no choice in the matter but to respond in kind. Based on history and a few educated guesses about future Soviet, Chinese, and U.S. behavior, this arrangement appears to be the most likely: the one best suited to U.S. global interests and most likely to protect ASEAN in a dangerous global environment. However, it is not a very attractive future for ASEAN or for us. It presupposes that the U.S. policy will be consistent and that the country will be willing to provide security leadership for East Asia generally. This approach would almost certainly provoke Soviet efforts to meet the challenge, admittedly on unfavorable terrain and terms. The arrangement would remain highly vulnerable to opinion shifts in

China and Japan, as well as in individual ASEAN countries, as each came under increasing pressure from Soviet threats or cajolery.

By the alternative approach the United States could adopt a more subtle policy that would permit ASEAN to set much of the tone for Southeast Asian developments while the United States provided a security backdrop (as one of several external participants in a balance of power), knowing that some day it might be asked to decamp from a "zopfanized" Southeast Asia. Such a strategy would also involve gradual development of relations between the United States and Vietnam, something that neither side would find easy. We have already been pulled in different directions by Chinese and ASEAN priorities during the dispute at the 1981 UN General Assembly over the role of the Pol Pot regime in Kampuchea. Since ASEAN and China have fundamentally different ideas about Indochina's future, a policy of following ASEAN's lead could strain our relations with Beijing.

Considering short-term goals, we hardly have a choice. The current situation in East Asia is very much to our liking, and we have little reason to change our policies. Only from a long-term viewpoint is the alternative attractive because it promises less pressure on U.S. resources; a security system based on the regional—and hence more stable— situation; an alternative for Hanoi's dependence on Moscow, thereby excluding rather than containing Soviet influence in Southeast Asia; and, some reassurance against a possible change in Chinese policy. These long-term advances take on added weight if the future is viewed in terms of the global trends.

In fact, not many policy choices are now open to us, no matter which kind of future we decide to work toward. We could, however, change our emphasis by keeping options for Vietnam open wider, by showing a preference for ASEAN over Chinese leadership when Kampuchea becomes an issue, by toning down rhetoric that makes our profile higher than necessary, and by deemphasizing our global concerns in Southeast Asia and thinking about alternative arrangements for our global security requirements.

We have been fortunate in Southeast Asia until now, probably to a greater extent than our earlier performance there merited. A major lesson of Vietnam for the United States was that Southeast Asia, though important, is not vital to our security, and it is an area in which we do not need to be a dominating external force. Even considering Soviet presence in Vietnam, the sea routes through the area are hardly likely to be threatened, except in a widespread military conflict. Regional states show considerable resilience, their nationalism is strong and purposeful, and, though their concern over the Soviets is not always as vehemently expressed as is ours, they share our preference for sharply limited Soviet involvement. In formulating policy for southeast Asia we have considerably opportunity for flexibility and imagination; despite our substantial interests, it is a place where we can afford to take some risks.

South Asia

South Asia[3] presents a very different picture from Southeast Asia. Although Afghanistan is arguably part of a West Asian system and Burma could be included in either South or Southeast Asia, the subcontinent is generally a well-defined system behind defensible borders. The long period of British dominance, which affected even nominally independent nations of the subcontinent, provided a degree of historical unity. Important ethnic, religious, and economic factors (including level of development) tie large parts of the region together, and, until shortly after independence, it was generally expected that a unified India would be the successor to the regional Pax Britannica.

India, however, became independent in two parts in 1947, and since then two dominant facts have overshadowed the region. First, India possesses an overwhelming regional preponderance far beyond anything that Indonesia could hope to enjoy in Southeast Asia. By almost any measure, India is more than twice as large as the rest of South Asia combined; the Congress-dominated political system has been stable to a fault; it has pursued a generally steady foreign-policy line with determination if not always success; and, it has developed a military machine of great regional dominance as well as a nuclear capability.

Second, an uneven rivalry exists between India and Pakistan, itself a candidate for middle-power status. In any other part of the world, Pakistan would be regionally dominant because of its size, its military capabilities, the exceptional skills of its diplomats, and its economic potential. In its neighborhood, however, Pakistan is overshadowed by its huge neighbor. Too small to rival India even if it could mobilize support from all other subsystem members, but too large to willingly yield place, Pakistan has become a disruptive element in the South Asian subsystem. The situation is aggravated by the extremely bitter split between the two countries and the long-lasting disputes between them, notably over Kashmir.

Since independence this system has been defined by conflict and unrest. Pakistan, as well as Nepal, Afghanistan, Sri Lanka, and Bangladesh, would much prefer to be located somewhere else, away from India, much as Mexico and Canada would be more comfortable if they had more distance between themselves and the United States. Even if India were a thoughtful and generous neighbor—which is sometimes the case—the system's imbalance is simply too great for comfort. In earlier years enmity between Afghanistan and Pakistan further complicated the situation, but it has now become subsumed in a much larger problem.

Not surprisingly, Pakistan and the smaller system members have sought to offset India's predominance by looking outside the system for allies, whereas Indian policy has consistently been to prevent outside intrusions, which it regards as direct challenges to its primacy. The most notable intruder was the United States. In the mid-1950s, for reasons of global diplomacy that hardly took note of South Asian dynamics, we allied ourselves with Pakistan, and India responded with a looser, but still close, relationship with the Soviet Union. Somewhat later, Pakistan realized that the U.S. tie was insufficient and made common cause with China, which was glad to become involved because it had bilateral problems with India and because it could thus strike a blow against the Soviet Union.

The affairs of the South Asian subsystem thereby became intertwined with the major global system in both of its manifestations: U.S.-Soviet and Sino-Soviet rivalries. Two wars between India and Pakistan—the second of which resulted in the breakup of Pakistan and the establishment of an independent Bangladesh—coupled with this high degree of intrusion from the global system, completely shattered any systemic unity within South Asia itself. Occasional attempts by Nepal, Sri Lanka, and even Bhutan to find external patrons clouded the picture still further.

The degree to which the Soviet Union would be able to exploit its position and establish dominance over South Asia became a critical question. Both the United States and China had reduced their security involvement substantially after 1965, leaving Moscow an almost free hand and, because of its increasingly close ties with India, an apparently better position to achieve hegemony in South Asia than in any other part of the world except Eastern Europe. Moscow's use of this status, especially in the late 1960s, was instructive. At Tashkent, the Soviets effectively mediated the aftermath of the 1965 war, and they became a much greater stabilizing force in South Asia, seeking to maximize relations with both Pakistan and India rather than playing the latter off against the former. In the process they both irritated the Indians and failed to satisfy the Pakistanis, much as the United States has done in similar circumstances.

The principal obstacle to Soviet hegemony in the region was India's ability to maintain its own position of leadership. Despite the 1971 Indo-Soviet Friendship Treaty, India was able to fend off threatening Soviet advances. New Delhi's success rested mainly on its own strength, its growing ability to dispense with Soviet assistance as perceived threats from China and Pakistan (and indirectly the United States) lessened, and ultimately the maintenance of a U.S.-Soviet global balance that provided India with freedom to maneuver. Economic ties to the United States also remained important to India and indeed to all regional states. The United States was a direct source of aid, the dominant voice in international lending councils, and an increasingly important market. Since South Asian nations are among the world's poorest, these relationships had to be tended carefully; the Soviet Union was in no position to replace them, although it did make some significant economic contributions to India.

Tangible U.S. interests in South Asia itself are slight (except for our transregional concerns to the west). The region is insignificant to our economic dealings, especially now that it no longer depends on food imports. South Asia is the pole of ultimate indifference to us geopolitically, and there is nowhere Americans want to go that takes them by way of South Asia. Although some close personal attachments have been formed between Americans and South Asians, there are probably less of these than with any other populated region of the world. Our initial humanitarian concerns persist but for many reasons have waned. Although Pakistan was an important element in the ring of containment around the Soviet Union, our concern diminished as containment became first irrelevant and then unfashionable. The level of threat to these modest interests is also very low—at least until the Soviet presence in Afghanistan is solidified.

Those who assert the importance of South Asia to the United States fall back upon the region's size, the relatively advanced sectors in its economy and society, and the not inconsiderable argument: What would the world look like if the Soviets dominated such a huge part of it? Moscow, in contrast, can demonstrate a very strong interest in South Asia on geopolitical grounds: The region is near some very sensitive sections of the Soviet Union and remains important as a part of the Soviet containment ring around China. Psychologically, the Soviet Union finds the India tie important because Soviet diplomacy has had few successes in developing warm ties with independent countries. If the Third World were divided into spheres of influence, the Soviet Union could mount its strongest claim in South Asia.

From the late 1960s, South Asia was largely a Soviet preserve. The United States was preoccupied with Vietnam, the opening to China gave our Asian policy a new focus that ran counter to prickly relations with India, and after a herculean effort in getting food to famine-threatened India in the late 1960s, the importance of the aid relationship faded for both Washington and New Delhi. The low level of interest in South Asia was ironically the reason for one of the most dramatic moves the United States has ever made there. When Henry Kissinger sought in 1971 to deter India from dismembering Pakistan, through a show of military force in the face of what he perceived as a Soviet-instigated power play, the audience was in Moscow and Beijing, not in South Asia, and few would claim that his actions made much sense in terms of the realities of the situation in South Asia. This intervention is one of the great examples of unfettered U.S. globalism and was a luxury that Nixon and Kissinger could afford precisely because of the very low place that South Asia held in their global priorities.[4]

However, South Asia fared hardly better under quite different circumstances, for despite Jimmy Carter's genuine interest in the Third World generally and India in particular, his relations with South Asia were also overshadowed by global concerns. Nuclear nonproliferation cast a heavy pall over our ties with India and largely immobilized our relations with Pakistan. Human rights was a secondary but significant impediment to our relations with Pakistan and Bangladesh. The global policy of restraint in arms sales was added to the menu, along with several other global policies. Indeed, South Asia is probably the locus classicus of the impact that the "new" global issues had on U.S. policy toward a significant region of the world.[5] The point was clear: Whether in terms of traditional security issues under Nixon and Ford or of the new global order issues under Carter, South Asia policy was overwhelmingly determined by considerations that had little to do with the region itself.

South Asia seemed, however, to be moving toward greater internal stability during the 1970s. The 1971 war had brought home two important facts to Pakistan. First, India could not be bested on the battlefield with conventional weapons, and dreams of gaining Kashmir through military means were empty. Second, despite the rhetoric of Kissinger and the Chinese, no outside power was going to run serious risks to its own security on behalf of Pakistan. Even the shah of Iran, a close ally of Pakistan, sought to diversify his position by improving ties with India and urging Pakistan to be conciliatory. India was now a formidable power in its own right, and the limited treaty arrangement that it entered into with the Soviet Union in 1971 served as a further prop to its status.

India also learned something: The 1971 treaty had drawn it too close to the Soviet Union to be compatible with India's view of its own stature and nonalignment, and, more important, the Soviets could not now do much for India. New Delhi had established its own predominance on the subcontinent, and Moscow, not Washington, was its potential rival. As I have noted, India's need for Soviet military support had greatly decreased, and the increasingly sophisticated Indian economy no longer found the Soviet Union a very useful source of assistance.

Thus, both India and Pakistan focused on regional problems in more constructive ways than they had in the past, and they showed signs of wanting to reach a modus vivendi rather than of looking for outside support. Progress was very slow, changes of government in both countries complicated matters, and no routine mechanisms were established for carrying on discussions among the South Asian nations. The Southeast Asian nations had been learning how to talk with each other in ASEAN, but even the most routine interstate connections among the South Asian nations were almost totally absent.

The United States welcomed this modest movement toward regional understanding. Kissinger had quietly come to terms with the post-1971 situation in South Asia, and Brzezinski explicitly included India among the nations he expected to provide leadership in regional affairs. Given the fairly low level of U.S. interest in South Asia, the United States did not much care how the system functioned as long as the region remained independent of Soviet control. India was now the only candidate for leadership, and the Morarji Desai government (1977–1979) showed that it recognized the wisdom of exercising its role with grace and sensitivity. Desai, even more than Indira Gandhi, saw that a more balanced nonalignment was important if India were to play an effective international role. Both Desai and Gandhi continued to emphasize the need for good relations with Moscow, so the Soviets also found the arrangement minimally satisfactory. If their grandiose commitment to India had not brought spectacular rewards (access to naval bases, support for Brezhnev's Asian security proposals, and a role for the Indian Communist party), the situation was still favorable, and they too had little choice but to play along with India. For the first time since the 1950s, the South Asian system seemed headed toward autonomy based on a rough balance among the global powers but at a low level and on grounds defined from within the system itself.

This situation was quickly undermined by renewed push from the global system. The lesser intrusion came from a shift in U.S. policies. Even before the promulgation of the Carter Doctrine, U.S. concern about the Gulf was growing. As we will see in the next section, by the late 1970s the United States had acquired a vital interest in oil from the Gulf, an interest under serious threat. Our interests in South Asia changed very little, but because of its location the region assumed a much greater role in our global strategic concerns. U.S. involvement was heightened by the ties that India and Muslim Pakistan had to some of the Gulf states, as well as by the increasing U.S.-Soviet competition in the Indian Ocean. By the early 1980s, South Asia had moved considerably higher on the U.S. list of priorities; again, however, this move resulted from global reasons unrelated to the region itself and had a deadening effect on our sensitivity toward the regional powers' interests, such as India's unhappiness over sharply increased U.S. naval presence in the Indian Ocean.

An important event in determining U.S. policy toward South Asia was the Soviet invasion of Afghanistan, which brought into question the rationales of all parties involved in the region.[6] Pakistan was most severely affected: Waves of Afghan refugees fled across the border, and for the first time a significant military force appeared in Afghanistan. More ominous, a pincers movement, effected by Soviet forces in Afghanistan and India (a Soviet ally in the view of many Pakistanis), would have had the capability to snuff out the remains of the Islamic state. Although most outside observers discount a joint Indo-Soviet threat, Pakistan's concern was understandable. Islamabad was faced with another difficult decision when the Carter administration executed a complete about-face following the Soviet invasion and pressed assistance and de facto alliance on a Pakistani government with whom only weeks before relationships had reached a bitter nadir. Pakistan found itself pressed on one hand by an ominous threat, and on the other by an offer of friendship that—based on U.S. refusal to come to its aid in 1965 and 1971—it had good reason to mistrust.

India was hardly less discomfited. Its regional aspirations—a position of leadership with Pakistani acquiescence and a near exclusion of outside intruders—were shattered overnight. The arrival of Soviet troops in the subcontinent reduced India to the position of second strongest power in the region. India's position was further undermined as both Washington and Beijing offered extensive assistance to Pakistan, and the United States proposed a relationship that would inevitably reintroduce it into the security affairs of the subcontinent. The Soviet invasions also triggered a much more active U.S. posture throughout Southwest Asia and the Indian Ocean, further impeding Indian primacy in its wider neighborhood. The South Asian system was again swept up in the global power struggle, but unlike in earlier decades, both India and Pakistan had good reason to be chary of involvement.

The morning of the invasion should have presented Jimmy Carter with an ideal opportunity to put regionalist theory into practice: Rather than calling President Zia ul-Haq of Pakistan to offer aid he could have contacted the prime minister of India to comment sympathetically on India's problem and express the United States' concern, but emphasize that India had to take responsibility for dealing with it. Had Morarji Desai still been prime minister, this tactic would have been an excellent approach. (Whether Carter, or any U.S. president, could have shown such steely nerves is another question.) Through a stroke of extremely bad luck, however, the Soviet invasion coincided exactly with Indira Ghandhi's resumption of power. Indian policy was immobilized, and the visible signs pointed toward acceptance of the Soviet action. Only over the course of several months did India extricate itself somewhat from its diplomatic ineptitude and give the impression that it realized the enormity of what had happened. Even then, concerns about Muslim extremism and warm ties to the Soviet Union ensured that New Delhi never strayed far from the Soviet line.

Pakistan's response was more skillful. President Zia held the U.S. offer of aid at arm's length until Jimmy Carter had departed the scene, and he set to work mobilizing support for Pakistan's position at the United Nations, among the nonaligned nations and especially in the Muslim world. His success was much greater than the United States and its allies could have ensured on their own, just as ASEAN provided legitimacy for the Kampuchean cause outside the cold-war context. By maintaining distance from the United States and by professing a desire for a rapid but just settlement of the Afghan problem, Zia somewhat assuaged Indian concerns about Pakistan as a channel for reentry of U.S. security interest in South Asia. Although the two governments still indulged in competitive rhetoric, increasing numbers of Indians and Pakistanis began to recognize that their region was in danger, and, more important, that this danger could be averted only if India and Pakistan set aside their differences in the face of the greater threat.

At the same time several smaller regional states sought to defuse the situation and incidentally to gain maneuvering room for themselves. They were particularly concerned about the latter following the return to power of Indira Gandhi, who had been better known for wielding sticks against her neighbors than for offering carrots. Bangladesh, which had begun to develop an international and diplomatic personality, took the lead in calling for wider regional cooperation, and the other regional states also saw advantage in dealing collectively with India. The Indians easily discerned the motives behind proposals for greater regional cooperation, but the initiatives were difficult to fend off. Who, after all, could refuse to attend a block party? Although Pakistan might have seen some virtue in a regional ganging up against India, it too was skeptical of a regional arrangement, fearing that India, with its great size and seemingly unlimited supply of skilled personnel to staff any secretariat, would overwhelm the other members. Furthermore, subcontinent partition, not unification, was Pakistan's raison d'être. Bangladesh persisted, however, and modeled its plans on ASEAN. By limiting discussions to economic and cultural affairs, by proceeding with small steps, and by reassuring all concerned that decisions would be made only by consensus, Dhaka disarmed some fears of its large neighbors. After a series of preliminary meetings, the South Asia Regional Cooperation (SARC) forum was launched at a meeting in New Delhi in August 1983.[7]

If SARC is to prosper and if the South Asian nations are to cooperate in developing regional autonomy, an essential element would be exclusion of the superpowers from the security management of the region. Some U.S. hopes for closer military cooperation with Pakistan as part of a strategy to protect Southwest Asia from Soviet encroachments would have to be abandoned.[8] Similarly, Moscow would have to set aside its aspiration for closer security ties with India. Both Washington and Moscow would have serious reservations about regional cooperation. For the Soviets, limitation of access to South Asia would be a more serious loss because South Asia is the one area in the Third World where the Soviet Union enjoys a position of leadership and sees its interests as predominant among the outside powers. For the United States the problem is less pressing, since South Asia is so distant and relatively low on the U.S. scale of interests. Had the issue arisen a decade ago, the United States undoubtedly would have warmly welcomed any arrangement that promised to isolate South Asia from the U.S.-Soviet competition and to relieve it permanently of security involvement there.

The United States would even now find the situation unacceptable only if it decided that access to Pakistan was critical to its ability to pursue its interests in the Gulf. This decision, incidentally, would rest on three assumptions: (1) that the United States needed Pakistani real estate for air and naval bases, (2) that these bases would actually be made available in a crisis, and (3) that, left to their own devices, Pakistanis would not make a contribution of equal value to Gulf security. Islamabad has, in fact, consistently played a very useful role vis-à-vis the United Arab Emirates and Saudi Arabia. Close association with the United States could undermine its political strength in the region and among the nonaligned and Muslim groups, and in all likelihood it would impel the Indians to work counter to U.S.-Pakistani interests in the Gulf.

A close tie between the United States and Pakistan would almost certainly have to include an automatic commitment of U.S. support if India and Pakistan again became embroiled in hostilities. This tie would, in turn, greatly strengthen the claim of Indians who argue for a definitive commitment to the Soviet Union. Any policy that forges a common front between India and the Soviet Union can hardly be considered a success in South Asian terms: As we and the Chinese have both learned over time and the Soviets knew from the beginning, the stake in South

Asia is India. A policy that accepts the risk of losing India can be justified only in terms of extraregional benefits of extraordinary importance and value. In contrast to Southeast Asia, the subcontinent does not offer even the theoretical opportunity for the United States to play a leading role in organizing regional security; even with Chinese support we could assert our position only at prohibitive expense.

A more attractive balance involving autonomous, regional security management could be attained only through cooperation among India, Pakistan, and the other South Asian states. The United States can do very little in a positive sense to bring about the kind of cooperation in South Asia that would produce these results. We could, however, have a tremendous negative effect if we inserted ourselves into South Asian security matters through close ties with Pakistan, through a posture in the region (including the Indian Ocean) that New Delhi found threatening, or through a highly visible and active policy that thrust Afghanistan further into the East-West competition. Any such intrusion would introduce uncertainties and divisiveness into the system that would make cooperation unlikely.

Despite occasional promptings and initial overenthusiasm directly following the Soviet invasion of Afghanistan, we rejected these courses of action and our restraint (seconded by intelligent Pakistani policies) has been beneficial to the modest beginnings of regional cooperation in South Asia today. A further positive step has been the U.S. decision not to become directly involved in the confrontation between Tamils and the Sinhalese majority community in Sri Lanka but rather to look to India to provide political leadership.

These promising trends are, however, even more vulnerable than their counterparts in Southeast Asia. SARC, at its best, remains hostage to Indo-Pakistani cooperation, and despite some modest signs of rapprochement (in conjunction with the SARC summit meeting held at Dhaka in December 1985), Rajiv Gandhi has yet to extend his innovative and imaginative style of problem-solving to Indo-Pakistani relations. The nuclear problem lurks on the horizon, and Soviet presence in Afghanistan remains a threat. India, however, has pulled back on its arms diversification policy and has placed huge new orders with Moscow, in response to U.S. military programs in Pakistan. South Asia could slip once again into a downward spiral of bickering, confrontation, and even war, sweeping aside the progress of the past decade.

If the United States wishes to support regional cooperation, it will have to forego actions that tend to exacerbate Indo-Pakistani relations or introduce global problems further into the region. Although we may protest that we do not intend to affect the internal power dynamics of the subcontinent, if the regional powers interpret our actions in those terms we will objectively become part of the problem, not of the solution. The steps we can take to promote cooperation will be very small, and they will not differ greatly from our current policies. We have little potential for pushing India and Pakistan toward resolution of their conflicts. The key to a successful South Asian policy for the United States will be to avoid taking counterproductive actions. That can be accomplished only if the United States decides what it wants to see happen in South Asia.

Middle East/Gulf Region

The Middle East, broadly defined, extends as far as Morocco and Pakistan, and Turkey and the Sudan.[9] The near universality of Islam, widespread use of Arabic, and shared history in the Ottoman and colonial periods, all provide some bases for such a definition. Michael Brecher's model of this region uses concentric circles focused on a core area comprising the Fertile Crescent states of Iraq, Syria, Lebanon, and historic Palestine and, less clearly, Egypt and Saudi Arabia. This area is indeed both the Arab and Muslim heartland, and events there have traditionally had repercussions far out into the periphery.

A far-flung Middle East is, however, as unwieldly in theory as in practice, and a more useful way of looking at the region is to see it as a series of subregions including Northwest Africa, the states around the Gulf and the Red Sea, and the Fertile Crescent core. In the following discussion, the term *Middle East* will be used to refer to this core area, the heart of the Arab world and the site of Islam's greatest challenge—the Arab-Israeli conflict.[10]

It is important to distinguish between these two aspects of the core area because the politics of pan-Arabism and intra-Arab relations in general has a past, present, and future independent of the existence of Israel. Although organizational expressions of Arab unity such as the Arab League have had little success, the ideal of unity is cherished among the Arab people and must be given at least lip service by any leader. Indeed, few regions have such apparent potential for cooperation and autonomy, based on both similarity and will for unity.

In fact, however, the Arab system is probably the most "penetrated" system in the world. Internecine quarrels, whether historic (Baghdad versus Damascus versus Cairo), dynastic, or ideological in origin, have mocked unity attempts, and the very factors favoring unity may be the greatest barriers to effective assertion of the less grandiose goal of regional autonomy. In a system where the dividing line between domestic and international politics is often blurred, each participant is highly vulnerable to subversive activities of its neighbor—activities often carried out in the name of the pan-Arab goal. Where differences of opinion are condemned by moral as much as expedential criteria, tensions can run particularly high, making the practice of traditional statecraft nearly impossible. Arguments within families are indeed often more bitter and difficult to resolve than those between business partners, and the demands and expectations of pan-Arabism are one of the factors that have overloaded the Middle East system.

Furthermore, no Arab regional influential has been able to impose cooperation. Egypt, under Nasser, attempted to but came up short and now stands aside from the Arab mainstream. Although several other Arab states (Iraq, Syria, Saudi Arabia) are important, none appears to have the potential for exerting widely accepted leadership, let alone hegemony. The Arab state system is distinctly multipolar.

The Arab world has another important spur to cooperation—the perception of a shared threat. Universally shared hostility to Israel should give the Arab nations a sense of threat and purpose rivaled only by the effect that South Africa has on its neighbors. This force has not, however, served to overcome the fundamental problems within the Arab system; often it has provided an excuse for failing to deal with them. A challenge to any system is useful only as long as it is not excessive, and Israel has repeatedly shown its ability to act at levels with which the Arabs cannot cope. The Arabs' military and political failure to attain their goals, despite apparently greater strength, has undermined their self-confidence. Thus the Israel factor too has become an overload on the system.

The existence of Israel as a perceived foreign element in the Middle East introduces the question of how the regional system is to be defined. The concept of an Arab system, standing in opposition to Israel, is an accurate reflection of Arab perceptions, desires, and goals. In fact, however, the Arab system is only an element of a larger Middle East core system that necessarily includes Israel. Israel sees itself as an intrinsic part of this region, and its close identification with the United States and Europe represents a failure in its regional policy. Israel would prefer a political future as the core of a Middle Eastern system in which it would be the engine of growth and development.

The Arab states reject this vision of the future. Even if dreams of pushing Israel into the Mediterranean have faded, the Arab world continues to see Israel as a foreign body to be isolated rather than incorporated. The unremitting hostility to Israel that provides an important (if flawed) binding force to an Arab political system makes the goal of a Middle East regional system unattainable. Unlike the ASEAN nations, which hope ultimately to bring Vietnam into an autonomous Southeast Asian system, few Arabs can envision coexisting in a system that would include full acceptance of Israel. For the rest of the world, however, the deeply bifurcated Middle East system, not the Arab system, has become the recognized regional unit, providing the terms of reference for outside involvement.

The kind of cooperation that would permit an autonomous Middle East region to set better terms of engagement with the outside world appears out of reach. The Arabs lack the strength to impose a regional solution that would satisfy them, and, aside from the peace treaty with Egypt, Israel has been unable to convert military victory into political acceptance. Frustrated by their regional failures and laboring under a profound sense of threat, each side has been obliged to look outside the Middle East for supportive relationships.

Meddling outsiders are hardly a novelty in the Middle East. As the Ottoman Empire declined, British, French, Russian and other nations staked out positions for themselves in the region. The achievement of independence after World War II should have provided the basis for substantial regional autonomy from outside manipulation, but despite some bright spots, regional autonomy remained an elusive goal. Nasser's overambitious attempt to rally the system around Egypt's banner raised the apprehensions of other Arab leaders, especially the conservatives who began to look for outside support. Their hour of need corresponded nicely with U.S. enthusiasm for alliance building. Washington had been unsuccessful in its attempt to enlist Egypt, just as it had been with India (for many of the same reasons). Conservative Iraq, along with Turkey and Iran (and Pakistan to the east), was amenable for its own reasons, however, and the Baghdad Pact was put together in 1955. Although the United States was never technically a member, the pact symbolized the United States' attempt to be the security manager of the Middle East.

The United States became involved in the Middle East for a variety of reasons. Like the Europeans, we valued the Middle East as a critical geostrategic area and the site of important oil reserves. In addition, it was a necessary element in the arc of containment around the Soviet Union, which had designs on at least the northern part of the region. The intraregional problems that motivated our allies (not only pact members but also those such as Jordan that were less formally associated with us) were of little interest in Washington. The outcome of ideological competition within the region was not in itself of great consequence, and Israel did not appear to be under serious threat. Whatever the U.S. motivation, however, the results were predictable, at least in hindsight. The United States became increasingly involved in the intraregional politics of the Arab and Middle Eastern systems, and the global rivalries were introduced into the area. Although Egypt was not overly worried about a U.S. role, it was concerned about the advantage accruing to its regional rival Iraq and turned to the Soviet Union for support.

The superpowers soon learned that establishing a position in the Middle East was much easier than turning it to advantage. The proclamation of the Eisenhower Doctrine in 1957, cast in terms of protecting the region against communism, fell on largely deaf ears since few of the nations were seriously concerned about Soviet aggression. The United States was embarrassed when the conservative Iraqi regime fell in 1958, and the landing of troops in Lebanon in that same year, though seemingly successful, was an event without positive consequences. The subsequent withdrawal of U.S. troops marked the end of active U.S. security involvement in the Middle East for the next decade. The Soviets found little more comfort. The Egyptians were much more willing to receive favors than to give them: Nasser spurned Soviet requests for naval facilities in Egypt, and Khrushchev's ardent courting of Egypt may have contributed to his downfall in 1964.

Even though the years between 1955 and 1967 were contentious in the Middle East, the Arabs were able to focus mainly on their internal problems, the prospects for regional autonomy were not critically undermined, and, from the U.S. viewpoint, the costs of involvement were not large. In 1967, however, the Arabs under Nasser's leadership set in motion a series of events that transformed the regional problems of the Middle East and its relations with the outside world. Almost overnight, the Arabs' internecine problems were reduced to secondary importance, and the two superpowers acquired stakes and incurred costs nowhere surpassed in the Third World. The war of 1967 and the Arab defeat by Israel brought home the full implications of the decade-old commitments.

Although the regional system of Arab states remained significant, the primary focus of all concerned was a Middle East system defined by the Arab-Israeli conflict. The interrelated problems of Israel and the Palestinians became central to Arab concerns in more than rhetoric. The role of Egypt shrank considerably, and pan-Arabism and the radical/conservative dichtomy became less important. As the Arab need for money to pay for arms grew, the role of the oil-rich states of the Gulf region took on new dimensions. Most important, perhaps, the Palestinians became independent and central actors. Since they lacked the traditional sources of strength and the responsibilities connected with status as a nation-state, they proved to be an especially disruptive element in the Middle East and further afield.

The results of the war brought home to the Arabs that they could not handle Israel on their own. In their immediate pressing need for new military equipment and political support, they turned with great urgency to the Soviet Union. Egypt now acceded to the Soviet request for bases; the Soviet naval squadron became a fixture in the Eastern Mediterranean; and in 1970, Egypt had to request the assistance of Soviet troops in fending off raids from the Israeli air force.

The war and its aftermath also marked the return of the United States as a full participant in regional security affairs. This time, however, its involvement was conditioned not primarily by intra-Arab affairs but by an open-ended U.S. commitment to Israel, a change with profound impact for our position far beyond the Middle East. Correspondingly, the Soviet Union broke diplomatic relations with Israel after 1967, thus seeming to complete the overlay of global polarization.

The polarization was not all that complete. Arab politics, if no longer central, remained active and provided some maneuvering room for the United States (e.g., support to Jordan when it was threatened by the Palestinians and Syria in 1970). Even though they were greatly dependent on the Soviet Union, the Arabs did not hesitate to pursue their own interests, and Israel was no less resistant to U.S. guidance. Indeed, the dramatic shift in the balance of power within the Middle East system did not result in any decisive shift in the relative influence of the United States or the Soviet Union; commitments only became deeper. Despite the significant changes in the Arab world, its remarkably stable nature was, if anything, enhanced.

The experience of 1967 could even have helped stabilize the Middle East system: It clarified the power realities that would have to be accommodated if a self-regulating, autonomous system were to be developed. The superpowers also seemed to favor a stabilizing settlement, and during the late 1960s actually favorable prospects for peace and autonomy throughout the region arose, if the necessary compromises could be struck. The moment of promise was brief. Israel, now the regionally dominant power, failed to capitalize politically on its military victory, preferring to hold onto the lands captured in the fighting rather than to use them to bargain for peace. It became increasingly isolated internationally, with costs paid in Washington as well as in Jerusalem. Both superpowers allowed themselves to be maneuvered into providing levels of support for their clients that transformed commitments into interests. The remaining Arab initiative was often preempted by the Palestinians who had their own agenda. By the early 1970s, the situation slipped into dangerous rigidity as the lines of confrontation hardened.

In the mid-1970s Anwar Sadat attempted to break through the systemic deadlock. The 1973 war was designed to shake Israel's complacency and restore some degree of confidence to the Arabs—or at least to Egypt. The subsequent reversal of Egypt's alliance was intended to change the nature of superpower involvement in hopes of furthering a regional settlement, and the trip to Jerusalem was made in part to preempt possible U.S.-Soviet imposition of a settlement of the Arab-Israeli conflict.

Sadat's brilliant grasp of regional realities and of the implications of superpower involvement gained Egypt substantial rewards. The other nation to benefit was the United States, for Sadat realized that the Soviet Union's usefulness was limited to supplying military equipment and making menacing gestures in times of crisis. Although these were important gestures, they could not bring the peace that Egypt needed. Henry Kissinger supplied the other half of the equation by excluding the Soviet Union from the peace-making process after the 1973 war. Although this move may or may not have facilitated the long-term prospects for peace, it certainly diminished Soviet interest in détente. It meshed neatly with Sadat's requirements and broke the pattern of polarization. In quick succession, the Soviets lost their ties to Egypt, drifted away from Iraq, and saw the PLO shattered—their previous position of strength in the Middle East core shrunk to a quarrelsome Syria.

The momentum provided by Sadat, Kissinger, and Carter was not maintained. U.S. attention wandered from the Middle East core as the Arab-Israeli impasse seemed less threatening and Iran-Iraq hostilities focused concern farther east. Without Egypt, the Arabs were split and the PLO fell victim to Israeli pressure and inter-Arab quarrels. Israel failed to turn Arab discomfiture to advantage, however, preferring to consolidate its security position rather than to seek further agreements. The United States, more and more preoccupied with East-West matters, increased the flow of economic and military assistance and allowed itself to be drawn closer into Israel's embrace, though unable to moderate Israeli policies.

The events in Lebanon refocused attention on the Middle East: Israel was badly damaged by seeking to assert direct control over Lebanon, and many U.S. political gains were eroded when it failed to retrieve the situation, demonstrating the limits of U.S. power and influence. The decimation of the PLO did not made Palestinians demonstrably readier to seek peace on terms acceptable to Israel, and the flurry of peace-making activities in 1985 showed little more promise than had previous ones.

In its broad outlines, the Middle East system, together with its external ties, continues to demonstrate features familiar to historians from earlier decades, even centuries. First, the system itself, which Carl Brown described as kaleidoscopic, is remarkably stable: The pieces shift dramatically and the patterns change, but the basic elements remain intact.[11] Neither the actors nor the issues differ greatly from what they were a decade or two ago. The central, Arab-Israeli issue remains intractable. The greatest change has been in the role of Egypt, but under Hosni Mubarak, Egypt is seeking to resume its place in the Arab firmament.

Second, the superpowers remain engaged, albeit with shifting bases of support. The U.S. and Soviet stars wax and wane and shift their relative positions but neither can displace the other. Each sees its vital interests engaged in this region as in no other part of the Third World.

Third, the influences of the global and of the regional systems are disproportionate. Both the United States and the Soviet Union have failed as regional security managers and as mentors of individual regional powers. Israel, Syria, Egypt—even Lebanon—are the most obvious cases of Middle Eastern nations refusing the guidance of superpowers and manipulating their patrons, confident that in the last analysis the superpower cannot stand aside and let its regional client be defeated (as the Soviets could have and we ultimately did in Vietnam). Either superpower might be willing to let a regional client pay the price of its adventurism within the terms of the Arab system (the existence of an independent Jordan, for instance, is not in itself of great concern to the United States), but in the core area of the Arab world, such matters also become important elements of the broader Arab-Israeli issue with inevitable global implications. It would be unthinkable for Washington or Moscow to permit the definitive defeat of the side it supported in the Arab-Israeli conflict so that external involvement serves to reinforce the homeostasis of the system.

The superpowers are unable not only to control the actions of their presumed clients but also to cooperate in imposing a solution on the region—even though they could between themselves easily agree on a basis for settling the Arab-Israeli problem. Their global rivalries prevent them from forming a condominium, and if they attempted to do so, their clients would make every effort to prevent it. Each superpower, however, does maintain the ability to frustrate any attempt by the other to arrange a peace settlement, at least as long as there is a regional state similarly disposed. Although the Soviet-Syrian combination is not that impressive, it is more than adequate to block U.S. peace initiatives.

Even if the United States and the Soviet Union were to work out and impose a joint settlement for the Arab-Israeli problem, they would necessarily continue their deep involvement in regional affairs as the coguarantors of the settlement. The possibilities for renewed conflict, if not between the Arabs and Israel, then within the Arab system itself, would be rich and varied, and neither Moscow and Washington would be able to let temptation pass.

The prospects then for an autonomous Middle East system—and by extension an autonomous Arab system—are bleak despite the undeniably positive factors. Although the combination of internal dissention and superpower concern may eventually be reversible, it is not a prospect in any period relevant to policymaking. Hence a policy of devolution with regard to the core area of the Middle East at least is not a realistic alternative.

This analysis cannot be automatically extended to the other subregions of the Middle East. They have their own interests that may or may not coincide with those of the core region. Most interesting for us is the subregion of the Gulf states. On one hand, its members have views on the Arab-Israeli situation close to those of their neighbors to the north and west. Two members are even more closely drawn into the affairs of the core area: Iraq necessarily plays a leading role in the affairs of the Fertile Crescent as well as the Gulf, and Saudi Arabia, the site of the Holy Places, is inextricably bound up with the affairs of the Arab and Muslim heartlands. Throughout most of the Gulf regions, large numbers of Palestinians, Egyptians, and guest workers ensure that the afairs of their homelands receive attention.

At the same time, however, the nations of the Gulf have become increasingly self-conscious and have learned to employ their wealth in ways that set them apart from the historic centers of Arab power. Their external relationships also contribute to a separate regional identity. The Gulf nations would prefer to avoid dependence on either the Soviet Union or the United States, but most of them recognize that their interests are better served in the short term at least by cooperative relationships with Washington and by considerable distance from Moscow. This approach is reinforced by their special economic interests, which draw them closely into the workings of the global economic system, both as suppliers of oil and customers for goods, services, and investment opportunities. Finally, most nations outside the Middle East have come to treat the Gulf as a district subregion.

The period of growing distinctiveness of the Gulf states has coincided with a time of greatly increased interest by the outside world. In the 1970s, the Gulf emerged as an area of literally vital interest to the United States—a third strategic zone in the global contest, along with Western Europe and East Asia. The Gulf's riches seemed to be rivaled only by its vulnerability, as sparsely populated, traditionalist states faced problems of modernization in conditions of extreme wealth. Fascination with the Gulf has receded somewhat with a decline in pressure on the international oil market, but that is a cyclical problem that will recur. It is unquestionably a region of major concern to the international system and will remain so probably even when its oil runs out because along with the larger Middle East system, it lies on a cold-war fault line, just as Southeast Asia does. In addition to the Arab-Israeli complex of issues, the Gulf system is also on the edge of other volatile systems— India-Pakistan and the Horn of Africa—and bilateral disputes such as that centered on the Yemens.

The composition of a Gulf subsystem has raised problems. On one hand, Saudi Arabia and the smaller Gulf states are particularly close in culture and historical experience, and they share a conservative political outlook. Traditional tribal rivalries have been largely set aside, and this group of small states offers particularly promising ground for a cohesive subsystem. They share the Gulf, however, with two much larger nations—ones that have passed through revolutionary experiences and would like to share those experiences with their brethren to the south. Iran and Iraq are the deviant members of the Gulf subsystem, and the long-term coexistence of small, immensely wealthy countries alongside fairly powerful nations with significantly lower per capita incomes is a critical problem for the subsystem. The day of reckoning has been postponed by the Iran-Iraq war, and ties built by the Saudis and other Arabs of the Gulf with Iraq might have lasting positive effect.

To understand the Gulf we must know what the nations of the region see as their greatest problems and what priority they assign to them.

• Iran and Iraq are, for the moment, each other's principal problem; thus they have been usefully diverted for several years. When they are through with each other, Baghdad has numerous scores to settle within the Middle East, and the Iranians may be tempted to resume the shah's course of empire. The problem of relating Iran and Iraq into a Gulf system is therefore a pressing one.

• For the conservative Gulf regimes, the main problem is maintaining themselves against domestic unrest that could be fomented by Iraq, Iran, and other Arab revolutionary elements, Palestinians or Communists, depending on time and place.

• Throughout the area, Israel is seen as a major problem, even a threat to the integrity of the Gulf region and of all the Arab world. Although we may find it useful to consider the Gulf subregion as an entity separate from the core area of the Middle East, as long as the Israel/Palestine issue remains unsettled, it will be a matter of profound concern for all Arabs and inevitably condition the way they deal with the outside world.

• Well behind these concerns comes the problem of the Soviet Union, which serves less as a direct military threat than as a source of subversion, although Iran is sensitive to special aspects of the Soviet threat, reflected in the 1921 treaty and the history of Soviet military intervention in Iran.

- There is also the problem of the United States, which is not only allied with Israel but is prepared to take unilateral action to preserve the flow of oil against any threat (including that from the oil's owners).

Formal cooperation among Gulf states has been late in coming. Before British withdrawal from its imperial responsibilities east of the Suez in the late 1960s, the issue did not arise because much of the Gulf was a British protectorate. Ever since, the distracting pulls of pan-Arabism, U.S. strategic involvement, and the separateness of Iran have all made formal cooperation difficult. For several years in the mid-1970s, an informal condominium between Iran and Saudi Arabia (the two pillars) promised to provide a structure that would also include the lesser Arab states of the region; only Iraq was excluded and even there the shah was pursuing conciliatory policies. Despite a considerable imperial aura, Iran's policies in the Gulf and toward South Asia demonstrated remarkable political leadership and diplomatic skill, qualifying the shah as one of the more exceptional international figures of this era. Unfortunately, money and time ran out, and the two-pillar structure tumbled along with the shah.

As Iran changed from a security support under the shah to a threat under Khomeni and as the U.S. hand seemed to falter, the Saudis and Gulf Arabs realized that they must look more to their own capabilities to supplement or to replace support from outside. The Soviet threat, even in the light of Afghanistan, contributed relatively little to their reassessment. The formal expression of concern was the Gulf Cooperation Council (GCC), formed in March 1981 by Saudi Arabia, Kuwait, Bahrain, Qatar, the United Arab Emirates, and Oman. The GCC has not received much publicity or international attention. In negative terms it is a conglomerate of weaknesses. All participants have monarchical governments with questionable futures, modernization pressures have not yet reached full force, and the population base is small. The group's total population is less than a good-sized U.S. or Asian metropolitan area, and most members must rely on imported labor, some of which is potentially subversive. From a positive viewpoint, the system remains well oiled with money, and most of its leaders are astute politicians who understand the internal and regional problems facing them and are making intelligent attempts to cope. Although members have different outlooks and emphases, they recognize the need to minimize the roles of the superpowers, they are particularly chary of Soviet subversion, and they share a broad common outlook on the world. The system has risen organically with no prompting from the outside; it makes good sense.

Like ASEAN, the GCC cast its early efforts and most of its public image in economic terms. Aside from quiet subventions to less affluent members (which have long been a feature of Gulf politics), the GCC has made progress in facilitating investment and movement of labor among its members, and it has begun efforts toward joint planning of industrial and other undertakings to avoid further wasteful duplication. Important opportunities for similar cooperation in the security area have arisen in the integration of members' defense systems, several of which are based on highly sophisticated weaponry purchased from the United States and Western Europe. Under growing pressure from the Iran-Iraq war and perturbed by the growing prospect of superpower involvement, the GCC in 1984 formed a more explicit security system. In November 1984 it set up a small rapid reaction force that, while having limited capabilities, could be useful as an alternative to outside involvement in minor crises. Most important, cooperation could come in the area of greatest threat, in which help from outside is of no avail— the danger of subversion that moves easily from the north across the borders of the GCC members.

Even if its members survive subversion and other internal problems, the GCC would have to face the related issue of how to engage Iraq and Iran in a cooperative dialogue. Hostilities between the two have provided valuable breathing space for the GCC to organize, and both Saudi Arabia and Kuwait have shown considerable skill in finding a limited basis for cooperation with these regional deviants. Much of the potential for a successful engagement would depend not only on how well the GCC pulls itself together but on what Iraq and Iran look like after their war and after the Khomeini leadership ends in Iran.

Whether regarded as a unit or a series of individual states, the Gulf region has not become the power vacuum that most outsiders had expected only a few years ago. The region's nations are approaching their problems purposefully, and their apparent decision to avoid close association with either superpower is encouraging, as is the reduced danger that their mutual differences will cause them to call in superpower help that could polarize the region. The GCC could develop into an important interlocutor for the entire region and a shield for the smaller members that find it difficult to stand up alone to outside presure. These, however, are matters for the future; at present the GCC is more a promise than a reality and may not offer much more than the sum of the individual capabilities of its members. The future of Gulf security is still wide open and remains a major cause for concern to the other nations of the world that are so dependent on it for oil. No matter how adroitly the Gulf states play their hand, their future will be in large part determined by the interplay of forces that they can hardly affect, let alone control.

Although the results of the influence of outside powers has been mixed, on balance they have been helpful. On the negative side, the Soviet Union's regional aspirations are worrisome. The spillover of Arab nationalism and radicalism fed by Arab-Israeli conflict is potentially explosive, although the Saudis and other GCC members generally play constructive roles in the larger Arab world and thereby help their own cause. On the positive side, Gulf states can count on diplomatic support from the Europeans and Japan and, in certain situations, might receive useful security assistance as well. More important, several states in neighboring regions provide a larger context for the Gulf, insulating it from some outside pressures and providing valuable security assistance. Both Pakistan and India have strong interests in regional security; Pakistan provides important military aid to Saudi Arabia and the United Arab Emirates and has close ties to Oman. India is less directly involved but keeps open useful lines of communication to both Iraq and Iran. Jordan and Egypt have important ties to the region, and the latter provides a potential avenue of access for U.S. forces. Although none of these is decisive alone, they are cumulatively important. Combined with an imaginative GCC policy and against the background of U.S. global capabilities, they could provide the basis for much more positive evolution of the security situation in the Gulf than would be the case if the Gulf members were at odds with each other and could only turn to the superpowers—which would mean for most the United States.

Although the United States has declared that the Gulf is vital both to itself and to the economics of developed countries in general, First World countries are not the only ones interested in the area. The Gulf region is a concern in Moscow because of geography and perhaps in the long term because of oil. Gulf nations are nearer to Soviet territory than is much of Central America to the United States, and unimpeded access to the ports of the Gulf would be very useful to the Soviets for economic and strategic reasons. The cold war spilled over very early to the region; during World War II, Soviet troops had occupied northern parts of Iran and were withdrawn in 1946 only under U.S. pressure. Although the Soviets have had little influence on the littoral countries of the Gulf because of the complexion of governments there, they enjoy some strong positions near the Gulf in Yemen and the Horn of Africa, and they maintain a significant naval presence nearby. Following the enunication of the Carter Doctrine and the earlier breakdown in U.S.-Soviet talks about arms limitations in the Indian Ocean region, Brezhnev and other Soviet officials forcefully demanded a voice in the affairs of the region and contested the right of the United States to play the leading security role there. The December 1980 proposal for international guarantees that would include the Soviets got nowhere, but the chances of the Soviets' enhancing their position in the Gulf region are not unpromising. A host of opportunities are provided not only by the U.S.-Soviet competition and the Arab-Israeli dispute but also by numerous inter-Arab problems and the internal weaknesses of the regional countries. The Gulf region and the wider Middle East subsystem may be the most difficult areas for which to shape an accord that would accommodate Soviet aspirations in ways compatible with U.S. interests and those of the people of the region.

U.S. concern with the Gulf dates from the Truman Doctrine and the intervention on behalf of the shah in overthrowing the Mossadegh government in Iran in 1953. Our concern was not so acute then, however, because our interests were less vital (we were not dependent on imported oil) and the threat came only from a relatively weak Soviet Union. The level of power needed to dominate the Gulf region was small; the British managed regional security while the United States organized the ill-fated Baghdad Pact (later CENTO) in 1955, as part of the general containment policy. The members entered the alliance with little consideration for regional realities, the participants had widely varying interests and objectives, and the organization lived up to the dictionary definition of the word *cento,* which I assume, was unknown to the coiners of that acronym.[12]

The situation changed sharply toward the end of the 1960s because of the general reassessment of U.S. capabilities, the growth of Soviet power, other factors that led to the formulation of the Nixon Doctrine, and a change in the regional situation. The British decided they could no longer bear even this small remnant of the imperial burden and withdrew their presence, which had guaranteed external and internal security for the rulers of the smaller Gulf entities. In the wake of the events of 1967, Iran, Iraq, and Saudi Arabia were developing into more substantial international actors and would take quantum jumps with the changes in the international oil market. The 1967 war also intensified area politics, and potential internal instability was added to the Soviet threat. The overall threat was still low, however, and the U.S. policy response was creative and effective—the golden hour of the Nixon Doctrine. Rather than increase our own presence, we were determined to rely on Iran and Saudi Arabia to assume security management of the Gulf region, and for a while the two pillars were equal to the task. Removal of the British shield forced the smaller states to reassess their positions, and their responses were sensible. The global atmosphere was also favorable—low-level Soviet assertiveness and movement toward détente—although in 1969 the Soviets made their first significant naval deployments to the Indian Ocean.

Americans were comfortable with the situation, assuming that the two regional pillars were acting in U.S. interests. Although that may generally have been the case objectively, the shah pursued his own political and economic agenda. The latter turned out to be costly to us through increased oil prices, but the former was extremely effective because it was in the intelligent self-interest of a strong regional power, not something dictated from outside. The arrangement prospered and withstood the shocks of the 1973 oil crisis and of a January 1975 *Business Week* interview in which Kissinger asserted that the United States would not exclude use of force if regional states threatened Western economies with strangulation by cutting off the oil flow.

We faced, but did not really face up to, problems of new global issues in the Gulf. The shah's international skills blinded us to some of the realities of his domestic political situation and human-rights practices inside Iran. Ultimately, these realities were to cause the downfall of the shah and of our regional strategy. We ignored them for too long, and Jimmy Carter's mistake was less in proclaiming a human-rights policy toward Iran than in failing to do so consistently. Arms sales were an even greater problem. While strengthening regional powers, especially Iran, we virtually lost control over arms sales, thus undermining our image in the region and, ultimately, our ability to conduct an arms-supply policy anywhere, as public and congressional distaste grew. We also lost perspective on the nuclear issue; during the Carter administration's problems with Pakistan's nuclear program, the idea that the United States should promote a regional nuclear reprocessing arrangement between Iran and Pakistan was seriously canvassed on the assumption that Iran would be a stabilizing factor and could guarantee that Pakistan would not behave irrationally. Fortunately, the idea died an early death, but it reflected our inability to balance newer and more traditional global considerations in dealing with such a critical region.

The shah's fall was only one element in the new regional situation, and it came at about the same time as the reassertion of Soviet aggressiveness in the Horn of Africa and in Afghanistan. The possibility of a post-Khomeni takeover by Iranian Communists or direct Soviet intervention was even more frightening. In the face of this deteriorating situation and of the failure of regional arrangements to maintain a situation minimally compatible with our interests, the United States had to consider what role it could and should play in Gulf security management.

Our concern with the area is to some extent a reciprocal of Soviet interest, and we must also consider the Gulf as an element in the potential threat to Israel, to which we have a profound security commitment. By itself, however, neither consideration would warrant very active U.S. involvement in Gulf affairs without our global concern about oil.

Our interest is not the ownership of the oil and only secondarily the price and marketing arrangements. What is vital to us, along with other consumers, is that the oil continue to flow; in other words, that access be maintained and that regional markets be accessible so that we may recoup some of our expenditures on oil when the price is high. We also do not care greatly about the complexion of regional governments as long as they pump the oil at an acceptable rate. (Even Soviet-controlled governments would probably comply, but we could not take the risk that they might stop during an international crisis.) The region is not important to the United States in security terms, and we do not need to have facilities there to support our interests elsewhere. Aside from human rights (an issue on which we have very little leverage) and nonproliferation in Iraq, the new issues agenda is not critical in the Gulf. In sum, this is the exemplar of an area where our requirements are very narrow and limited to access.

Yet, if the flow of oil is truly a vital need for the United States and for our allies, can we take even a small chance that it could be turned off? Is the Gulf because of this narrow but critical interest an area in which access is not enough and domination must be secured? Distance as well as political factors, make access to the Gulf difficult, and even under favorable circumstances, the United States would face serious obstacles in trying to secure the area. Even in peacetime, we would risk depleting on-call forces by concentrating on the Gulf threat (a situation now being corrected), and our commitment to the security of the Gulf is an immense weight on our foreign policy. We have substantially mortgaged our policies to countries as diverse as Kenya, Morocco, Pakistan, the Philippines, and Egypt to support our position in the Gulf (some would add South Africa and hence almost all of Black Africa to the list). The implications for our position in time of general war are even more troublesome because the Gulf is not an area to which we would prefer to commit a substantial part of our forces in combat against the Soviet Union.

Our role in the Gulf region is undeniably precarious. Not only did the 1980 Carter Doctrine declare that the region was of vital interest, but in an October 1981 statement, President Ronald Reagan committed us to some extent to maintaining Saudi domestic order. To defend the Gulf the United States must reach to the extreme limits of the range of its military capabilities, for the Gulf is as far from us as the Falklands are from Great Britain, and stronger forces than Argentinians may wait on the other side—potential local hostility like that of Iran and a nearby Soviet army. Even if we could deploy military force in the Gulf, it is not clear what our objectives would be unless the Soviets are directly involved.

The picture also has its bright sides. Whatever its faults, the United States is more attractive to Gulf Arabs than the Soviet Union is, we have great political and economic influence, our global military capabilities are appreciated, and the sometimes fragile regimes of the Gulf states would like to have at least the option of calling us in. What they do not want is membership in a U.S.-led alliance, a public U.S. embrace, or a U.S. military presence directly associated with them. They cannot afford to be seen as propped up by foreigners who have a blatant preoccupation with their oil and whose association with Israel is political poison throughout the area. Even Oman has been careful to put public limits on its association with the United States, and proposals for a Jordanian force to be used for contingencies in the Gulf were undermined when Washington's hand in the affair became evident. The basis for a strategic consensus of the kind that Alexander Haig and to some extent Brzezinski hoped to achieve is simply lacking and will remain unattainable as long as the parties' priorities diverge so greatly.

In addition, formal agreements between the Gulf states and the United States may not be very useful in a crisis. The domestic political realities of the regional partner, rather than the U.S. perception of the threat, may determine whether the points of the agreement are upheld, for instance, whether the state permits us to use agreed-upon base facilities during a given crisis. Agreements entail at least implicit commitments that we are ill equipped to fulfill and that frequently harm the domestic and regional political position of our partner. Loose and tacit agreements are probably the most we need or can expect; there will be no strategic consensus, no CENTO, nor even a resurrection of a two-pillar policy under U.S. aegis. Secretary of Defense Caspar Weinberger's February 1982 offer of direct help to the GCC was rebuffed because members recognized that they and the organization must not be seen as agents of the United States. Although we share certain important interests with these countries, there are many that we do not share. An association built on that reality can be a strong one, but only as long as neither side expects too much of it.

Our purposes for involvement in the Gulf are clear. First, we want to deter Soviet aggression, something best done by relying on global capabilities with regional backup to prevent the Soviets from making unopposed moves (as in Afghanistan) and to force them, rather than us, to make escalatory decisions. Even if the regional states do not fully share our view of the Soviet threat, they are deeply concerned about it and appreciate the U.S. countervailing capability.

The second purpose for U.S. involvement concerns internally generated threats to the oil flow. Regional states again share our concern about internal subversive threats, but our capabilities to do anything about them are minimal. More problematic are the actions that regional states could take that would endanger the oil supply—either by a mandated cutoff (similar to that of 1973) or by internal or international war that might shut down Gulf production and shipment capacities. Regional states are well aware that if they cut off the oil supply, the United States will oppose them, potentially with force. This is a usefully sobering thought for them but also one that sets limits on the regional state–U.S. relationship because in the area of oil flow the United States is inevitably part of the problem. We likewise can do little about the danger of a shutdown resulting from regional hostilities except to reduce tensions (especially Arab-Israeli problems) that affect the region and generally attempt to lessen the tension. Here, too, effective regional cooperation through the GCC or other mechanisms must be the principal positive input.

The Gulf states have fared much better than we expected at the time of the Iranian revolution and the Soviet attack on Afghanistan and of the British withdrawal a decade earlier. The Iran-Iraq war has had only limited regional fallout. The United States has made an important but limited contribution to regional development; most of the credit goes to some quite astute regional leaders and their fat wallets. In the future, we would do well to allow regional states to define their own problems and, when possible, to take the lead in solving them. In situations in which we cannot follow their lead (e.g., Saudi proposals for dealing with Israel), we can listen attentively.

The U.S. position in the Gulf is stronger than might be expected. As we develop our skill in proferring security assistance, that assistance becomes more appreciated. Thus the establishment of Central Command (CENTCOM) to coordinate our security activities in the region was not met with fear and apprehension but was quietly welcomed. If the commander of CENTCOM must be based in Florida rather than in the Gulf, it is a small price to pay for regional acceptance. We have developed a more sophisticated sense of the Soviet threat and of the dangers posed by a fundamentalist Iran. The Soviets have not profited in the region: They have alienated Iran and Iraq, and their invasion of Afghanistan has caused a major setback in their dealings with the whole Muslim world. Soviet involvement in South Yemen and the Horn of Africa has caused considerable nervousness in Saudi Arabia and Oman. Although the Soviet Union enjoys a great advantage because of its proximity to the Gulf region, it is so close and threatening that alliance with it could not afford comfortable option if a regional dispute arose with the United States.

These considerations do not constitute a satisfactory grand strategy of the kind that Americans have always expected in areas where their vital interests are at stake. However, unless we are able to wean ourselves and our allies from dependence on Gulf oil, it is the best strategy available. Although our military capabilities in the region are limited, they may be adequate to meet realistic threats. Capabilities of regional states are modest but may be growing, and fortunately they are strongest in the areas in which we are weakest—dispute prevention and anti-subversion.

South Africa

In this section I shall initially address Africa[13] as an entity, although its states are too diversified to justify this approach. Common traits of poverty and underdevelopment have evoked some useful economic cooperation (the African Development Bank) and provided an initial framework for potential aid donors to think about Africa, but the economic realities are much too variegated to permit a continentwide approach. African nations come from a wide range of colonial back-grounds, and the colonial experience was too short to build the kind of common and effective structures that colonialists left behind them when they departed Asia.

The system's boundaries are geographically clear, but cultural dif-ferences deeply divide north and south, and the countries of the northeast quadrant have close relations outside the area, so that the Horn and Egypt-Sudan participate in world politics as Africans only to a limited extent. The Arabic-speaking states are also more or less closely tied into the politics of the Middle East. The remaining bastion of white supremacy in Africa, the Republic of South Africa, stands apart from the rest of the continent. Desperately desirous of acquiring a white, European, and northern identity, it plays a negative but highly important role in shaping whatever continentwide unity Africa can muster and has stimulated some very effective subregional cooperation.

Given Africa's lack of an objective basis for unity and its plethora of states and ministates, the continent should have been the scene of continual internal fighting. However, Africans have not only done a remarkable job of suppressing conflict but they also have achieved a useful degree of working unity on a number of political issues. This accomplishment is perhaps based on the time and manner of Africa's liberation from colonialism. Most of Africa's nations became independent within a few years, and few enjoyed independence before 1960. By 1960, the outside world had developed a positive, almost romantic view of the emerging nations, and Africa was invested with a special aura— one that the new African leaders exploited skillfully to reduce external pressure on them, whether from military force or other forms of intrusiveness.

The outside world was inclined to stand back from African developments and allow Africans to devise the continent's approach to the rest of the world. On one hand, the outside world was aware that many fragile entities in Africa needed breathing space to establish themselves; on the other hand, it felt a sense of guilt toward a continent whose human resources had been so ruthlessly exploited and a paternalism that survived from the metropole-colony relationships.

More important in shaping international attitudes, however, were the facts that African issues were not terribly salient to much of the world, that the continent posed no threat to anybody, and that outside nations had no desire to become enmired in African politics. Although this attitude provided breathing space, it also ensured that when regional crises did arise, the United States and the Soviet Union would view Africa in terms of global issues of the East-West confrontation.

The potential for East-West competition over Africa was not realized at first, because no real basis for contest arose until Soviet and Cuban involvement in Angola in 1975. The Soviet Union lacked the capability to project force into the region. Some political alarms did sound in the 1960s, as Khrushchev sought to make common cause with such supposed radicals as Kwame Nkrumah, Sékou Touré, or even King Hassan of Morocco. The high point of this period was the crisis as the ex–Belgian Congo became independent; cold-war issues were fought out mostly at the United Nations. For some fifteen years a Western security umbrella over Africa excluded some of the more direct forms of great-power competition. The necessary security maintenance that was beyond African capabilities was handled by the excolonial powers, France in West Africa and Britain in East Africa. (The fact that the former metropoles could continue to play a quasi-imperial role in parts of Africa is vivid testimony to the low level of security capabilities on the continent itself.) Although this arrangement was not ideal for Africans, it spared them from much of the tension in the global system, and it provided them with important opportunities for developing and maintaining a greater degree of autonomy than might have been expected.

The vehicle for asserting African autonomy was the Organization for African Unity (OAU). The OAU necessarily suffered from all the weaknesses of the continent that it represented. It was too big, it lacked focus, and it was divided along numerous fault lines. In short, the organization did not correspond to an existing or logical international subsystem and was thus extremely limited in its aspirations. The OAU was based on the fiction of a united Africa; it lacked the ability to turn that fiction into reality.

Like Africa, however, the OAU did more than expected. It expressed the newly free continent's desire for autonomy and for some degree of interstate stability. The OAU helped advance the propositions that Africa could handle its own problems and that an outside power should not intervene except at the specific request of an African government. For many years, any rivalries among Arican states were resolved or contained without resort to warfare between nations or to extensive intervention by one state in the internal affairs of the other. The OAU served to bring pressure on the outside world to promote the few issues on which African nations could agree (mainly aid and apartheid). Thus, by the criteria applied to evaluate a regional organization, the OAU deserved decent marks.

During the past decade or so, Africa and the OAU have confronted a series of challenges that they have been unable to meet on a conti-nentwide basis. Outside forces, not just Cubans but also Americans, Soviets, and French, have been increasingly involved in security problems as mediators and as suppliers of military assistance and through direct intervention. Although Libya and South Africa are African nations and the former is a member of the OAU, both have increasingly acted to disrupt African unity and African security, and the OAU has been largely helpless to deal with them.

Although outside forces have been assuming responsibilities that Africans should be performing, the nations of the continent have managed to preserve a modicum of autonomy. Even when the OAU was more influential in resolving interstate African problems, its role was often indirect. African leaders recognized early that they were more likely to achieve results by delegating the OAU's responsibility to smaller groups of states directly concerned with specific problems. This technique put responsibility on those whose interests were most at stake and who were most familiar with the situation, and it removed from the picture those who were comfortably distant from the danger and who would use the situation for irresponsible grandstanding (as Idi Amin did on the southern African question in 1975). The OAU provided a useful, umbrella-like function by endowing the delegated group with an air of legitimacy and by maintaining the African mystique. In reality security maintenance had to be entrusted to smaller subsystems, and realization of such subsidiarity is certainly the beginning of wisdom for bodies such as OAU when dealing with an area as vast and diverse as Africa. The African subsystems are still in the early stages of development and differentiation from each other and from the overall system. Although their potential is open to question, they can provide an important focus both for the settlement of African problems and for outside powers dealing with African reality.

In a continent where almost all ties had been either very local or with the metropole, relatively little interchange had taken place among the component states of such logical subregions as the Horn, West Africa, or Northwest Africa. These separations persisted after independence, and only in recent years have intraregional exchanges—economic, cultural, political, and, to a lesser extent, security—become common. Most of these arrangements have been informal and de facto. The Sahel grouping came together in 1978 in response to a common catastrophe and the pressures of aid donors. A more formal grouping, ECOWAS (the Economic Community of West African States) was formed in 1976, but it has moved forward very slowly and has limited itself to a low-key role (rather as ASEAN did in its early stages). ECOWAS lacks the dynamism of ASEAN and its future is much less promising; nonetheless, it did develop organically in response to the perceived needs of its members. Presumably it has learned some lessons from its East African counterpart, which had a more promising economic base but was an artificial creation unable to stand up under diverse political pressures.

Another set of nascent groupings in Africa arose in response to crises and conflicts. Some of these are still engaged in working out their hostilities among themselves; others are attempting to cooperate against perceived threats from deviant members of external forces. The most striking examples of regional groups in conflict are that in the Horn (Ethiopia, Somalia, Kenya, Sudan, and Djibouti) and that in the Northwest Sahara (Algeria, Morocco, Mauritania, and Libya). Both sets revolve around would-be regional influentials, and both arose from disputes over inherited colonial boundaries. A third group is the Front Line states of southern Africa (Zambia, Tanzania, Zimbabwe, Botswana, Mozambique, and Angola). which are cooperating in the face of problems associated with white minority rule in southern Africa.

Although several African states have the potential for becoming regional influentials, most must first put their internal houses in order. Nigeria, the most promising influential, has already played a significant role in West Africa (notably in the Chad crises of 1979 and 1982) as a leader of the African bloc in the United Nations and even on matters pertaining to southern Africa. With its mix of weakness and promise, Nigeria is perhaps the quintessential regional influential. Reeling from economic and political blows, it has played a less prominent international role in the mid-1980s, but as long as it remains a united country, it will inevitably play a leading role in West Africa and beyond.[14] South

Africa is undeniably a regional influential in that it wields substantial economic and political influence over its neighbors, despite its apartheid policy. Pretoria seeks to establish a constellation of southern African states—a compelling idea. Until South Africa fundamentally alters its domestic policy, however, the republic can at best enforce its will in limited areas and play the role of regional deviant.

The challenge of white supremacy in southern Africa has evoked the most effective regional response in the entire continent—the Front Line grouping.[15] This informal caucus developed in response to decolonization issues in Mozambique and Angola, and in 1976 it received a delegation of authority from the OAU to deal with the Rhodesian problem. It rapidly became the effective interlocutor not only for "Africa" but also for the liberation movements in Zimbabwe (and later in Namibia) in their dealings with the outside world. The Front Line group has consistently sought to preserve regional autonomy in the face of threats from an increasingly powerful South Africa and from the intrusion of the U.S.-Soviet rivalry. In the latter, they have been remarkably effective. The Soviets, having nothing to contribute except a threatening mien to compel U.S. attention, have been kept at a useful distance on political matters. Moscow has not been able to insert itself into situations that it must see as among the most promising for its interests, and the Front Line has used the pressure of the African bloc at the United Nations to keep the Soviets from disrupting peace moves sponsored by the West with Front Line support. The Americans, valuable interlocutors with entrée to white regimes, have deftly been kept involved as have the British. As the Rhodesian situation neared its denouement, the Front Line was able to gauge the pressure that could usefully be applied to Washington and London and was realistic about its own capabilities; overall, its diplomatic performance was impressive in an extremely difficult situation.

The modus operandi of the Front Line is very informal and flexible, and it points up the group's lack of structure and support. The group is composed solely of the presidents of the concerned states, and it relies on their considerable personal rapport. Several Front Line leaders, however, do not sit too firmly on their presidential chairs, the ideology and philosophy of their regimes differ greatly from one another, and several of the individual states are fragile. Problems faced by the Front Line have become increasingly difficult, and the degree of pressure on individual states has changed over time. (Tanzania has not been physically on the front line of anything since the Portuguese left Mozambique.) The group has been less successful in dealing with the Namibia issue than it was with Rhodesia, and it has not yet found an effective direct approach to the apartheid problem, its most difficult issue to date. The attitudes of Europe and the United States are more ambivalent than they were on the straightforward decolonization issues, and the liberation movements within the republic present a difficult dilemma. The moral case for supporting the Front Line is undeniable, but the ability of Pretoria to bring pressure on its neighbors is equally real. The future of the Front Line is cloudy at best.

Yet the Front Line is the only available alternative for African autonomy, and the international community as well as its members has a stake in its existence. To encourage unity and resist the tremendous economic pull of the republic, the Front Line has formed an economic grouping—the Southern Africa Development Coordination Conference—that has successfully attracted outside economic support. In 1980, the countries of this grouping concluded an informal defense agreement and are cooperating on internal security matters related to South Africa. This attempt to provide added dimensions to a regional subsystem is far from success, and the economic, political, and ideological problems are immense. Still, a number of the diversities that bother outside observers may not bother Africans as long as ideologically inclined members refrain from trying to export their ideas. Some of the ideological differences may be abating, as Angola and Mozambique look to the West for economic support and Tanzania begins to face the shortcomings of its policies. If a new generation of leaders can muster a degree of statesmanship similar to that of their predecessors, the Front Line group has at least a fighting (or, better, nonfighting) chance of remaining a critically important element in the security of a very sensitive part of the world.

To say that the Front Line group is the most promising security grouping in Africa is a sobering thought. The other nascent groupings in Africa have not had similar opportunities to develop and test themselves and have tended to wax and wane as crises have arisen and passed. No other grouping has been able to face up to a significant threat either from an intrusive outside power or from a regional deviant (witness the continuing Chad problem). Major disputes in Northwest and Northeast Africa remain far from accommodation. Although Africans have been fairly successful in resisting unacceptable levels of outside intervention, the continuing roles of the United States, France, and Cuba in the continent's affairs symbolize Africa's partial failure to preserve autonomy.

The overlay of U.S. policy on the African background is no less shifting and uncertain. Africa has traditionally vied with South Asia for the lowest priority in our ranking, only to be catapulted for brief periods into the glare of excessive attention. The one area in which our interest has been traditionally high, the Republic of South Africa, cannot by its nature provide a lasting, positive policy focus for the United States. However, it still commands a devoted following, whose most creditable reason for concern is its strategic location on the cape sea route and its natural resources. More recently, as our concerns in the Middle East have risen, an upsurge of interest has occurred in the access routes across northern Africa and the Indian Ocean littoral of the continent.

Although Nigeria and other countries on the west coast of Africa are significant sources of oil for U.S. and European markets, our economic interests in Africa are dominated by a concern over development of some of the poorest and hungriest parts of the world. Like most of U.S. development concerns, however, this one is inadequately supported with resources and development assistance and must compete with security assistance needs. The handling of human rights in much of the continent has been an embarrassment to Africans. Some of the most egregious situations in Black Africa (in Equatorial Guinea and the erstwhile Central African Empire) have been improved, and the most flagrant case in Idi Amin's Uganda was handled regionally when Tanzania moved in. Continuing poor standards of treatment of individuals and a widespread absence of democracy in Black Africa make it more difficult to argue against the South African apartheid system, which in theory, and often in practice, is the most appalling human-rights situation in the world.

Among the other new global issues, arms sales (including our own) to the continent continue to raise problems, and the South African nuclear potential is a persistent concern. The sheer mass of African votes in the United Nations is a matter of interest to a small number of concerned Americans. For the most part, the approach of U.S. policymakers and the general public has been one of disinterest, and their interest has been stimulated only occasionally by crises. Pressure for a more regionally sensitive policy is the province of some business-people, liberal groups, and church groups. The black community's concern has only recently resulted in significant policy input.

Within the U.S. government, conduct of African relations in noncrisis periods has been left to the lower-level bureaucracy concerned with political and developmental issues. This heavily regionalist approach, combined with lack of broad interest, has resulted in a U.S. policy of disengagement from African political and security affairs in hopes that the Soviet Union would remain similarly disengaged. African could have provided a useful model for superpower restraint and for autonomy from the global system.

Moscow was unwilling to play the game, however, and a series of crises within Africa and in the nearby Gulf propelled African affairs to the purview of poorly prepared senior U.S. leaders and forced policy toward Africa into global contexts. The Congo crisis of 1960 provided a foretaste of this approach, and it came into its own in the late 1970s in response to developments in Angola and the Horn. In the interim, however, when even major African events were free of East-West implications (the Nigerian civil war, for example) the United States remained on the sidelines. Also the Carter administration made a serious attempt to deal with Africa, as indeed with the rest of the Third World, outside the context of East-West rivalry. Throughout most of that administration, they approached Africa in terms of such global concepts as human rights, arms transfers, and development economics. (When things went sour in northeastern Africa in 1979, however, policy toward Africa slipped back inexorably into a U.S.-Soviet framework that was passed on to the Reagan administration.)

U.S. involvement in Angola was a horror story of globalism; in concept it was much worse than in Vietnam.[16] The story began when the United States supported the Portuguese colonial position in Africa, seemingly against the entire logic of U.S. political values and common sense. Acceptance of the Portuguese role in Africa was the price that the United States paid for use of air bases on Portuguese territory, the Azores. Costs of relocating air facilities are tangible and immediate, global threats are somewhat less so, and the benefits of better relations with Africans are long term and vague. Faulty global considerations prevailed over regional ones in a classic example of why a regionalist presumption should influence our policymaking.

The next stage of events (in 1975, the Portuguese had decided to withdraw, and rival groups were contesting for power in Angola) was hardly more edifying, as regional realities were again ignored. The United States had been backing an Angolan faction in a small way, apparently because the Soviets were backing somebody else. We focused much more on the provision of arms to the combatants than on the political forces at work, and we failed to hand the matter to the OAU for a possible regional arrangement. Incredibly, we failed to understand that association with South African intervention would make our position completely untenable. Genuine concern among Africans about the Soviet and Cuban role in Angola was overshadowed by a force that appeared to them much more threatening and evil. Although the U.S. government knew the facts of the situation and they were recognized at high levels as valid theoretical propositions, they were disregarded because of our global approach to an overwhelmingly regional issue. Predictably, as our side lost ignominiously, the South Africans and mercenaries had to retreat. The Cubans and their Soviet backers gained an ascendancy they never could have aspired to if we had stood aside. The United States suffered a major global setback because the Soviets' ability to mount a challenge over large distances, never before tested, was broadcast to all. U.S. policy of détente with the Soviets was dealt a severe blow. Finally, we badly misjudged our own domestic situation by assuming that the U.S. public and Congress would support, so soon after Vietnam, an adventure so divorced from our interests. In the final blow to U.S. policy, Congress prohibited any further activities in Angola—a major blow to the U.S. presidential power.

As a superpower the United States has a considerable margin for error, a latitude that came to our rescue in the longer term in Angola. In a testimony to the powers of a capitalist economy, the United States maintained a broad range of options with regard to Angola. Although Cubans can fight battles, they are not very useful in convincing South Africa to leave Namibia or in building a viable economy (the Gulf Oil Company does a much better job on the latter point). Also, there is no reason why the United States cannot have a mutually beneficial relationship with the Angolan government in bilateral and regional terms. Unfortunately, the global cloud continues to hang over the relationship because of the determination of the Carter and Reagan administrations to give priority to the Cuban element in the Angolan equation, a connection that has also worked to the detriment of a Namibia settlement.

Another positive outcome of the Angola fiasco was that it was informative for Henry Kissinger and most other Americans who had missed the point about the changing situation in the Third World. The Angola crisis demonstrated that Africa had outgrown the imperial system and that the Soviet challenge had become global. Thus when the next crisis arose (the transition of white Rhodesia to black Zimbabwe), Kissinger listened to advisers who pointed out that U.S. regional interests would be best served by a realistic settlement in Rhodesia and that the United States should associate itself with the cause of majority rule, lest the proponents of that cause call upon the Soviets and Cubans. This globalist formulation carried the day, and Kissinger launched a process that ultimately would prove vital to British success in bringing a viable settlement to Zimbabwe. In the process, the United States and the West in general were able to strengthen our credibility and position in Africa as a whole and with the Front Line states in particular.

The important points of the Rhodesia negotiations are that the United States (1) allowed regional forces to play a major role in shaping a solution that met regional requirements and (2) played its own global role in the background—which was less a matter of blocking the Soviets than of leading a global climate of opinion that forced white Rhodesia to accept the inevitable with a minimum of disruption. Working with the British and the Front Line presidents, the United States demonstrated its value as an intermediary while removing the conditions that would have led to Soviet and Cuban military involvement. Despite a very difficult domestic situation in the United States, the Ford and Carter administrations wrote some of the brighter pages of U.S. diplomatic history in the Third World, not because of idealism but because of simple pragmatism in picking the winning side.

Angola's lessons suggest some possible policy approaches for other parts of Africa in which the pull of global concerns is particularly strong. The United States is not very worried about who controls large stretches of the western Sahara Desert or whether Morocco or Algeria organizes the security of northwestern Africa. The outcome of the quarrel between Ethiopia and Somalia and other political issues in the Horn are also of secondary importance. U.S. interests in Zaire might perhaps be better served in the long run by a change in that country's leadership. In all of these cases, however, global considerations have drawn us into regional problems inconsequential to our interests. The degree of U.S. involvement and the importance of the global factors vary, and no easy judgments can be made on the wisdom of U.S. policies.

U.S. involvement with Morocco has little to do with Africa. Like the Philippines, Morocco provides useful facilities for the rapid movement of U.S. forces to the Middle East and the Gulf. Although we have supported OAU mediation of the western Sahara question, we have associated ourselves with King Hassan in his regional struggle with the Saharan tribes and, ultimately, with Algeria in its contest for regional leadership. In the process we risk aligning ourselves with the weaker side of this region, and we may impede the evolution of a realistic and stable Northwest African regional system.

Somalia, a regionally disruptive power, overreached itself in contesting with Ethiopia. Originally it was aligned with Moscow, and when that tie was broken, the Carter administration declined to move in. Not only was President Siad Barre regarded as an unpredictable associate, but also there was some sentiment, even following Angola, to demonstrate that we would stand by the terms of the 1972 Moscow agreement and not seek unilateral advantages.[17] For similar reasons, the United States stood back in 1977, when major disruptions occurred in the Shaba province of Zaire, despite allegations that these were fomented by Cubans from Angola.

In a short time, however, the situation in Africa changed. The use of Cuban forces and Soviet materiel in Ethiopia broke the regional mold in the Horn. Even more significant, both Somalia and Kenya became important sites for facilities that could strengthen the U.S. military position in the northwest quadrant of the Indian Ocean and the Gulf. After the fall of the shah and the Soviet invasion of Afghanistan, these considerations took on overriding importance. Although the degree of importance of these facilities and their availability in time of real crisis are arguable, if their importance is granted, it is surprising that the United States has been restrained in associating itself with Somalia. In any case, we have entered a regional situation in which our associate has been trying to revise colonial borders (an illegitimate task by African standards) and is the weaker party in an area dispute in which we have no direct interest.

To round out the picture, much the same forces in Zaire's Shaba province replayed the 1977 scenario one year later. Our involvement was noticeably greater than in the first Shaba unrest even though the French, Belgians, and Moroccans carried most of the direct burden. The predominance of the regionalists among Carter's advisers had not lasted very long, and African issues again became functions of global problems.

It can be argued that a global approach is the best strategy for handling Africa. The continent does not function as a political unit, and since its northern sections are more parts of the Arab world, it is reasonable to treat them as such. The Soviets have not showed much restraint in their African policy, and their association with the Libyan regime cannot be ignored as Muammar Qadafi seeks to interfere in the affairs of all states in northern and even central Africa. By the same token, Namibia and Angola are important to the United States because of their relationships with Cuba and with the Soviet Union. The Republic of South Africa is valuable because of its potential role in meeting Free World mineral requirements and in protecting the cape sea route. Morocco and nations of the Horn play similar parts. Pan-Africanism is a mirage of the nostalgic past, and regional focuses within the continent are tenuous and not very important to the broader U.S. interest. The problems in Africa should be dealt with in political and security terms because they relate to important U.S. global concerns; we can safely ignore the protests of those Africans who are unable to play a significant global role and who therefore want to focus attention on their continent.

Stated so baldly these arguments are distasteful, but they are not necessarily wrong. Although early Carter policy was warmly welcomed in Africa, it could not withstand the cold wind of political reality. If Africa is drifting leftward, the United States can expect little from cultivating regional and bilateral relations anyway. Our economic attractiveness either will or will not be adequate to carry the day, but it will have to do so on its own.

The familiar counterarguments are equally compelling. It makes little sense to alienate a continent: As long as Africans want to be seen a unit, we should oblige them. Our past forays into regional contests have often turned out poorly, and no evidence suggests that we would do better now (and nothing suggests that we could successfully maintain the fiction of noninvolvement). Also, though the concerned U.S. black community has done a very inadequate job of lobbying government on behalf of African interests, it has demonstrated greater skill on the South Africa sanctions issue. No administration would want to alienate it unnecessarily. The government continues to need policies that would both prevent Soviet involvement in the South African denouement and provide us with some guarantee for continued, favorable access to South Africa after the event. A globalist approach can postpone the day of reckoning, but it cannot offer a positive outcome. South Africa would be happy to participate in a U.S.-led global consensus but not if it involved the end of white supremacy. Globalism, narrowly defined, would ineluctably lead the United States to association with apartheid, with morally devastating implications and with long-term, possibly very high political costs.

The alternative to a hard-core, globalist position is too often taken to imply an acceptance of reality as defined by Africans and their partisans within the United States whose judgments overcompensate for the sins of the globalists. The Carter administration could have much more easily conducted an effective and balanced policy in Africa, for example, if more Africanists in the Department of State and elsewhere had understood the broader Soviet threat and the domestic perception of that threat.

A sensible middle ground does exist between the globalist and regionalist extremes, one that recognizes the validity of both, accepts the fact that U.S. interests in Africa are quite low, and admits that this premise can equally well lead to the relegation of African affairs to the global or to the regional arena. Different approaches might be followed in different places or at different times but under the general assumption that regional processes should be preferred unless the globalization of a problem is clearly essential. To the extent possible, it makes sense for U.S. policy to identify with the more reasonable African aspirations (as the Carter administration did originally) while policymakers look closely at the possibility of greater reliance on the emerging regional groupings under an overall OAU umbrella. We are not deluded here: These regional groupings have far to go to prove themselves effective, and the United States can do little to strengthen them. We will be called upon perhaps repeatedly to become involved in African affairs, either as a mediator or a participant, and some calls will have to be heeded. However, if Nigeria or even France were to take the lead, for instance, in settling the Chad problem, we would do well to let them try. Much agony is in store for southern Africa; our first concern is not to share it. Our second concern is to work with—or at least not to impede—others who seek a just solution.

Central America

In almost all regards, Latin America has a much stronger basis for unity than does Africa.[18] The region is linguistically nearly homogeneous, its nations share common historic and cultural traditions, it is at least as self-conscious as Africa, and it has more experience in regional cooperation. The Latin American nations have had a different kind of exposure to imperialism and thus a longer tradition of statecraft and diplomacy than have African countries; yet the final result in the two systems is not very different. The Organization of American States (OAS) and the region as a whole have not fared much better than the OAU has in solving disputes, in excluding external intrusions, and in building durable and effective institutions. Some reasons for these shortcomings are common to both systems: Both regions are too large and too diverse to form effective systems, and neither has faced the kind of common traumatic experience or external threat that can be so critical to unity. Behind the facade of established Latin American nationhood are conditions similar to those of recent colonial nations. Latin America has depended through much of its history on more developed parts of the world, its success in nation building (as distinct from the establishment of statehood) has been spotty, and it is saddled with a terrible ambiguity as a region.

As if Latin America alone were not a large enough unit, it is also part of a transregional construct that embraces the United States. The U.S. role in the hemisphere has varied substantially, but since at least the time of the Monroe Doctrine, the United States has assumed that it is the acknowledged and welcomed leader of the entire hemisphere. Generations of North Americans have come to believe that their ties to their southern neighbors are special. Our ideas of the physical relationships in the hemisphere are distorted: Most of us simply assume that Washington is much closer to, say, Buenos Aires than it is to Dakar, Tunis, or Moscow. At times, our feelings of a special relationship have seemed to be reciprocated, especially after World War II when the hemispheric nations formed the Rio Treaty for collective defense and the OAS—a stronger replacement for the Pan American Union. Through the 1950s and the early years of the Alliance for Progress, the hemisphere came to look increasingly like a coherent system: Economic relationships intensified, security cooperation grew, and the Western Hemisphere states acted as a voting bloc in the United Nations.

This hemispheric system was highly vulnerable. Weaker countries had always paid a price for U.S. concern—the price of U.S. intrusiveness if not intervention. Although the OAS supposedly had banned intervention (and the Roosevelt Good Neighbor Policy of the 1930s had already moved the United States in that direction), Washington continued to lay a heavy hand on hemispheric affairs, whether by berating the Argentines for their poor choice of leaders or by interventing directly in Guatemala in 1954 and in the Dominican Republic in 1965. Although the last action was tardily brought under the aegis of the OAS, it marked the end of the OAS as a security maintenance organization on issues of direct concern to the United States. The organization was able to perform useful services in settling the El Salvador–Honduras conflict of 1969 and the Peru-Ecuador fighting of 1981, but it has ceased to be either a useful tool for U.S. policy or a means for the other hemispheric states to limit U.S. intrusions.

From Washington's perspective, a principal function of the OAS had always been to exclude foreign intrusions, but in reality, for most of this century unchallenged U.S. hegemony provided this barrier. The shifts in power distribution that we previously examined undercut this function. Cuba was able to reach outside the hemisphere for support from the Soviet Union, and the hegemonic system was thereby critically breached. The loss might have been minor had the bulk of the OAS continued to accept strong U.S. leadership. But since we were no longer willing to support the anti-interventionist rationale of the OAS as it pertained to our own actions, other influential members were less willing to use it to prevent the kinds of intervention that we opposed. We thus found ourselves once again in a unilateralist role.

U.S. participation in the hemisphere's affairs became problematic for the other members as the hemisphere went through the same kind of de-imperialization process as did the rest of the world. The United States was not the typical imperial power and had never needed to exert direct control over any significant part of Latin America for any length of time. Our involvement in the de-imperialization process was also different: Unlike the European metropoles, the United States remained by far the dominant power in its former imperium. The basic pattern of change, however, was the same.

Hemispheric nations set about redefining their relations with the United States in response to the changing conditions. They asserted greater autonomy from U.S. leadership on international issues, involved themselves more in nonaligned and "southern" forums, developed economic and other ties with Western Europe and Japan, experimented with hemispheric functional groups that excluded the United States, cautiously resumed relations with Cuba, and explored ties with the

Soviet Union and China. More or less consciously they were seeking to redefine the hemispheric system by excluding the United States as a full-fledged member and offsetting continued dependence on the United States by establishing extrahemispheric ties.

Even without the United States, however, a Latin American system would be unwieldy. As in Africa, the outlook for regionalism seems brightest in smaller, more compact groups that share some common problems other than those arising from U.S. intrusion. Although Brazil and the Southern Cone countries (Argentina, Chile, and Uruguay) lack formal institutions and evince little cooperation except perhaps as regards security and intelligence, they have interacted extensively with each other, either cooperatively or in conflict, and they share a broad range of characteristics. They have generally succeeded in keeping external powers from exploiting their mutual differences (e.g., the Beagle Channel dispute between Chile and Argentina), and they have remained substantially independent from U.S. influence. For several years a more formal structure, the Andean Pact, made significant progress in promoting economic and political cooperation among Colombia, Ecuador, Peru, Bolivia, and Chile (Venezuela joined in 1973). However, the structure was undermined by a variety of problems, most of which arose from differing rates of political development in member countries.

Among the potential subregions within the hemisphere, Central America has the longest tradition of regional interaction and holds the greatest interest for current U.S. policymakers. Historically, the five Central American republics (Costa Rica, El Salvador, Nicaragua, Guatemala, and Honduras) have come closer to reaching regional unity than has any other Latin American group, and in the nineteenth century the republics briefly formed a confederation. Along with the Andean Pact, the Central American Common Market, set up in 1960, was the most effective economic union in Latin America, but it came upon evil days during the Honduras–El Salvador war in 1969. The logic of cooperation, if not union, is strong for these five small states, despite some fairly significant economic and political differences and disparities in size.

Present circumstances in the region provide little basis for a cooperative endeavor; the trend of events within Central America over the past several years has brought the region to international attention and created conditions both internally upsetting and externally inviting for intruders. Although Central America remains generally very poor and relatively backward by Western Hemisphere standards, the five small republics, as well as their larger neighbors, experienced rapid economic growth after 1970. This growth was not evenly distributed, and, together with a series of rapid social changes, it triggered opposition to the regimes in Nicaragua, Guatemala, and El Salvador, which ranked among the most sanguinary in the hemisphere. The potential for revolution and instability was rapidly approaching a critical point in these countries, and even Costa Rica and Honduras could not remain immune, despite their more open political systems. An additional blow was delivered by the global economic slump of the late 1970s and early 1980s. The overthrow of the Somoza dictatorship in Nicaragua and its replacement by a regime with close ties to Cuba raised the prospect of a dangerous cycle of intervention and counterintervention that would destroy what stability the region possessed.

The time may well have passed when a Central American regional system can be based upon only five nations. Recent events have polarized these states; the U.S.-Soviet global rivalry has impinged on them in ways with which they are unable to deal; and in the past decade other Latin American nations have become forces to be reckoned with by the Central American states, as well as by outsiders. First among these emerging powers is Cuba, which appears determined to make the dubious benefits of its social and economic system available to others in Latin America and beyond. Geographic proximity, cultural affinity, and a succession of events have provided Havana with ample opportunity. In itself the involvement of Cuba is of minor significance; however, the United States and several Latin American states are concerned about Havana's close ties with Moscow. Soviet involvement in Central America, even if indirect, is not only a threatening intrusion; it also automatically triggers a rapid and otherwise unwelcome growth of North American intrusiveness.

Cuba emerged as a prominent international actor because of changes in the international system. U.S. ability and propensity to intervene forcefully against deviant behavior were reduced, and other regional states gained a broader scope for independent action. Mexico, restive under the shadow of its northern neighbor, sought to put distance between itself and the United States. The oil boom of the 1970s, coupled with a decline in U.S. assertiveness, gave Mexico the wherewithal and opportunity to expand its role.

Venezuela's approach was somewhat different. In the late 1960s it developed a more assertive policy, based in part on concern that regional instability could both threaten the movement of its oil to distant customers and stimulate political discontent that could spill over to the oil-producing states. The political leadership in Caracas developed ties with like-minded Christian Democratic elements, especially in El Salvador, and used Venezuela's oil wealth to support useful trends in Central America some years before Mexico was able to do so. Colombia lacked the economic strength of Mexico and Venezuela and the political thrust of Cuba. It was deeply concerned about internal insurgencies, however, and because of its proximity and size it began to assert some say in the affairs of the region. Panama too began to take a more active part once its preoccupation with asserting sovereignty over the Canal was assuaged.

In sum, despite differences in approach and capability, a number of regional nations, sharing a concern for regional stability, have asserted a direct influence in the affairs of the smaller five countries of Central America, as well as in the Caribbean—in effect enlarging the original subsystem. Among them the belief is growing that radical change in the region is both inevitable and desirable and that Cuban, Soviet, and U.S. intrusions should be limited.

The United States did not stand by as revolutionary change gathered strength in the five Central American republics. As early as 1965, it attempted to promote a regional defense council, but this body did not survive the 1969 El Salvador–Honduras war. The Carter administration recognized the inevitability of change in Central America and took strong positions on human-rights issues, culminating in withdrawal of U.S. support as the Somoza regime lurched toward self-destruction. Carter made a sincere attempt to cooperate with the Sandinista-dominated government that replaced Somoza, and he floated expansive ideas of economic cooperation throughout the Caribbean Basin. By the end of his administration, however, relations with the Sandinistas had broken down over their role in El Salvador and their ties to Cuba, and Carter lacked the resources and political strength to move effectively on the development front. Relations with Mexico were strained, an immense amount of political capital had been consumed in getting the Panama Canal treaties ratified, and U.S. policy in Central America seemed to have come to a dead end.[19]

The advent of the Reagan administration forced a clearer definition of the issues. New plans for Caribbean Basin development were presented in July 1981 to a meeting in Nassau attended by the United States, Mexico, Venezuela, and Canada. (Colombia later was permitted to join.) In January 1982, Washington sponsored a Central American Democratic Community (CADC) consisting of Costa Rica, Honduras, and El Salvador. The CADC lacked broad regional credibility and never got off the ground, but the Caribbean Basin Initiative is just beginning to test its somewhat clipped wings. Although each program reflected an awareness that the Central American problem should be approached regionally, neither transcended the administration's double-barreled determination to maintain the U.S. role in the region and to demonstrate to a global as well as regional audience that the Carter days were past: The United States could and would take decisive action to protect its interests. Once again, global preoccupations clashed with regional imperatives in U.S.

policy to the detriment of the latter. As the level of U.S. rhetoric and involvement in Central America grew, Mexico and other regional leaders renewed attempts to head off still greater U.S. involvement and a possible confrontation between the United States and Nicaragua, along with its Cuban and Soviet patrons. The regional states were further concerned that the evolutionary or even revolutionary process in Central America should not again be frustrated by intrusions brought about by global competition as had occurred in Guatemala in the early 1950s.

Various manifestations of their concern came together at the January 1983 meeting of representatives of Mexico, Venezuela, Colombia, and Panama at the Panamanian island of Contadora. The Contadora Group implicitly set out to replace the United States as security manager by redefining the relevant region of Central America. All four countries have fairly impressive credentials in handling left-wing threats, in managing change in their own countries, and in playing roles independent of the United States, Cuba, and the Soviet Union. Although not a formal structure, the Contadora Group has found resonance for its ideas in Western Europe and within the United States itself.

The core of understanding among the regional states rests on two familiar propositions: (1) that Central America cannot be left on its own to sort out its problems and some kind of new regional order must emerge, and (2) that cooperation among the regional states is essential for curbing external intrusions. The Contadorists' ability to continue to work together toward these ends is questionable, as is their ability to achieve them even if they do cooperate. Mexico and Venezuela have serious weaknesses as potential leaders. Both are overshadowed by the United States, and their success depends substantially on Washington's acquiescence. Like Nigeria, both have had to engage in considerable sail trimming following the collapse of the oil boom. Panama and Colombia are stars of considerably lesser magnitude.

Until Cuba is fitted into a regional setting (the problem is analogous to that of South Africa, Vietnam, and Israel), a solution is difficult to envision. Dealing with Cuba is complicated by Havana's relationship with Moscow, as well as by its own desire to become a regional influential. Cuba is unlikely to take second place to Mexico, and the United States is unlikely to join Cuba as a coguarantor of Central American security. Keeping Cuba at bay and excluding it from Central American events will be difficult unless the social and economic situation in the region is extensively restructured—which is precisely the Contadora approach and the rationale behind it. It is not obvious what kind of internal restructuring within the Central American Five is possible, necessary, and sufficient, whether all five must tread more or less the same path, or how large a Central American region must be to provide an ample framework for containing regional problems while minimizing outside intrusions.

The most crucial variable in the Central American situation is U.S. policy. Many regional states see us as an intrusive power seeking to maintain an ineffective regional hegemony or as a more pressing threat to autonomy than the distant Soviet Union or Cuba which they believe they can ultimately domesticate. Washington's viewpoint is of course different: No Third World region is as close to the United States and none has acceded to U.S. hegemony as extensively as did Central America. U.S. visions of hemispheric solidarity, the Monroe Doctrine with its various corollaries, and interventions in support of causes ranging from democracy to repayment of loans have all been focused on Central America and the Caribbean much more than on the remoter parts of the southern continent. Since the last century this region has been our imperium, and our dominance has been unquestioned.

The United States had good reason for establishing itself in the region. The five small states of Central America have hardly been models of stability, and the region itself is probably as vital to U.S. interests as any other in the Third World. Americans have recognized that a foreign presence in Central America would not only be discomforting but also could threaten the Panama Canal and our sea routes in the Caribbean. The United States also has substantial commercial interests in several Central American countries, although these are not critical to our national well-being. As the value of U.S. interests shifts over time, Central America may represent the limiting case for a U.S. policy of devolution that accepts regional nonalignment and restrictions on U.S. access. Central America may be the region in which, for both tangible and psychological reasons, we must play an active hegemonic role, as we have done in the past.

Despite its high level of interest, the United States has almost always been able to treat the Central American and Caribbean regions as policy backwaters. Our interests were not significantly threatened, and our capabilities were so overwhelming that we hardly needed to use them. As recently as the overthrow of the Arbenz regime in Guatemala in 1954 and the intervention in the Dominican Republic in 1965, the United States could assert its interests rapidly and cheaply, with acquiescence from other hemispheric governments. Yet even in these two examples the seeds of decline in the U.S. position are evident because they were reactions to a new threat perceived by Washington—Soviet involvement in this hitherto protected preserve. For the first times in recent memory, Central America became an object of serious U.S. strategic concern because of its relationship to a global threat.

The policy of the early Carter years was focused on the global issue of human rights as it pertained to Central America and the way that the region related to broader North-South questions. U.S. concern about oil supplies from Venezuela and Mexico triggered an additional policy concern in Washington that also involved a global, not a regional problem. An important but lonely exception to this trend was the U.S. decision to move ahead with the Panama Canal treaty.

As we have observed, Central America is a somewhat special case in the general decline of U.S. (and other metropoles') ability to project their power into the Third World. The United States retains the un-questioned physical capability to invade Central America, defeat any opposition on the ground, and occupy the region for some period. In a small way we demonstrated this capability in Grenada. Any larger undertaking, however, might be militarily costly and politically unpopular at home and abroad. In a country where an anti-American revolutionary movement was deeply rooted, we would either have to undertake a long-term, social transformation or expect that the same problems would reappear in more virulent form after we left. Even in Central America the center/periphery relationship has changed. Pressure on the Sandinista government in Nicaragua has still not compelled its leaders to make major policy changes; much less effort was effective in toppling Arbenz.

Although we cannot know what specifically the Soviets and Cubans intend to do in Central America and how they intend to go about it, they are unquestionably up to no good in terms of our interests. Likewise, there is little question that Central America's period of unrest can afford the Communists important opportunities for further mischief. Given the threatening potential, the United States must decide how best to protect its interests, whether through

- direct intervention
- a policy of regional leadership that would seek to join Central American strengths to those of the United States in pursuit of solutions defined by the United States
- a policy of devolution that would look to Mexico and other area nations to play the leading role in managing regional security

There are no straw men among these options. If the combination of interests and threats is critical and other alternatives are lacking, we would be foolish not to act decisively. The second option has provided the general framework of our recent policies and represents an attractive mix of approaches, but it relies on the existence of a political center that may no longer exist in large parts of Central America. It also suffers from an internal dilemma: In the current political atmosphere, U.S.

attempts to provide leadership, if not backed by congress and convincing resources, tend to mobilize as much opposition as support in the region. Those hostile to us react to a perceived threat; those with regional aspirations want to fend off advances that could limit their growing freedom to maneuver. Adroit fine-tuning may still turn this approach into a winner, but on the basis of past performance and given the many pulls on U.S. policy, it is difficult to be optimistic.

The devolution option should also be considered seriously. All parties agree that some kind of regional political and economic context is mandatory for solving Central America's problems. From the U.S. viewpoint, isolation of the region from the East-West framework is essential, and in theory a strong regional association could effect this separation more economically than the United States could do unilaterally. As long as the United States is regarded by many influential Central Americans as the principal threat to their autonomy and independence, automatic openings will exist for the Soviets and others to exploit. However, if the regional states feel strong enough to deal with us on a basis of equality and security, their temptation to turn to outsiders would diminish. Although Mexico may have reached this level on its own, the smaller nations and revolutionary groups in Central America and the Caribbean will probably only find confidence in a broader, regional arrangement. This arrangement could also provide the framework for addressing the Cuba problem rooted in East-West confrontation. Breaking Cuba loose from its Soviet alignment is a long-term prospect, but effecting it would be more likely if Havana felt secure vis-à-vis the United States within a strong autonomous region.

The Soviet Union cannot realistically expect to support a series of clients in Central America given the situation's economic and military realities. The United States will never be a negligible quantity because of its proximity and close economic ties. We should use our policy to help Central America regard the United States as a guarantor against Soviet and other unwanted intrusions rather than as a threat. Given the history of our relations with Latin America, it is difficult to see how we can play such a role unless we stand outside a reasonably strong and self-confident regional system.

Although our capabilities may have declined in Central America, we still can frustrate the development of an effective regional system. We now face the question of whether we want to use that capability. To do so we can employ simple tactics: We can cast issues in an East-West framework, resist eforts to bring deviants into more cooperative relationships with system members, and undermine regional initiatives for settlement. Although some of our more recent policy moves could be described in these terms, it is unlikely that we have followed a considered plan to prevent evolution of a regional system. We have taken these actions for other reasons, but they have in effect weakened moves toward regionalism.

The United States must also consider whether the regional states would be able to restore basic stability and exclude Soviet and other hostile intrusions. Even if they could, would a solution that sharply restricts our own access to the region be compatible with our interests? In the earlier discussion I noted some weaknesses of the regional system and its principal actors; the Central American situation does not inspire great confidence. As to repelling intrusions, it is not certain or even likely that the long-term objectives of Mexico or other regional nations are fully compatible with our own. Yet we cannot judge the seriousness of this problem without a clear view of our own minimum interests in Central America and a better understanding of the possible outcomes of regional interests.

It seems unlikely that the highest levels of U.S. government have realistically considered what our future role in Central America should be. Must we be the dominant, hegemonic force? Can we limit our access in direct proportion to the neutralization of Soviet, Cuban, or Nicaraguan threats? Would we find the role of guarantor or over-the-horizon supporter of the system's autonomy satisfactory? The answers to such questions are nowhere more elusive than in Central America, and in no other region would the United States find it so psychologically difficult to face the devolution of security management.

However we answer these questions, we must remember that the United States sees more in Central America than merely various initiatives of regional states that more or less oppose our goals. It sees the emergence of a regional subsystem, whether called the Contadora Group or something else, and if we fail to relate to this system on its own terms, we will make our own objectives in Central America much more difficult—probably impossible—to achieve. Finally, we must recognize that the trend in Central America is part of a larger process of the devolution of power and responsibility taking place in the entire Third World.

We may well be able to stem the tide here and now by our unilateral actions. That approach would be expensive, however, and would require a strong act of national will. If we could avoid these stresses by understanding the historical processes involved and skillfully adapting our policy to them, we would be well advised to do so.

7.
POLICY DIRECTIONS

W E HAVE CONSIDERED THE challenges presented by the Third World
and explored some broad strategies for meeting them. In this final
chapter we shall consider some basic factors that will shape U.S. policy
toward the Third World; redefine a concept that can be used as an
intellectual framework; set forth the elements of an overall strategy; and
see how these approaches can be applied to specific regions.

Obstacles to Policymaking

The keys to a sound U.S. policy for the Third World are much the
same as those for any part of the world; however, the emphases differ.
No policy is pursued in a vacuum, no matter what concept or strategy
the United States chooses, it must be one engendering support so that
it can be pursued consistently over time. Four elements are essential:

1. We cannot expect Third world nations to respond favorably to
our actions if we are not consistent and do not establish a pattern of
consultation with at least the most important of them. We must show
that our view of the future is consonant with their reasonable aspirations
and that it takes account of their interests and priorities and their
definition of regional issues. The Third World countries will also expect
us to play our role responsibly, both by supplying the global security
context in which the regional systems can work out their futures and
by allowing them to take policy initiatives with a minimum of interference. They will soon learn whether we will keep our part of the
proposed global bargain.

2. Our European and Japanese allies also need to participate in our
decisionmaking if their roles are to supplement ours. Although we have
effective consultation arrangements with them, we need to respond more

openly to their criticisms of our policies and recommendations for changes and to focus more on noncrisis issues in the Third World. Consultation means not only talking to others: It includes serious consideration of, and on occasion even acquiescence to, their preferences.

3. Most important, we must tend our citizens and the expression of their views in the Congress. Over the past decades, various administrations have offered a bewildering (and ultimately disillusioning) menu of reasons for U.S. involvement in the Third World that has substantially discredited such involvement. The public usually learns of specific Third World issues only when unpleasant crises arise; the Congress is regularly requested to supply funds for programs that have not lived up to expectations placed on them (e.g., aid has not stopped communism, ensured rapid growth, or made friends for us). Even Jimmy Carter never addressed the American people on broad Third World policy—an odd omission when so many of his policy priorities were in that area. If the public and Congress must defray the costs of U.S. Third World policy—whether military involvement in El Salvador, constructive engagement in South Africa, or return of the canal to Panama—they must be offered a framework within which to understand it.

4. Finally, we need to better control our rhetoric. We only strengthen the political impact of Soviet military capabilities in East Asia, for instance, when we exaggerate their relevant capabilities. By decrying as Soviet gains those changes that are really manifestations of Third World autonomy, we play into Soviet hands. When we seek political effect by asserting that our prestige or vital national interests are at stake in a given situation, we risk making this a dangerous and expensive self-fulfilling prophecy. Although much of this rhetorical excess is meant only for the U.S. audience it does not remain confined within our borders.

A major problem in U.S. foreign policy has been inconsistency. Our system tolerates a cacophony of foreign-policy views within an administration; our electoral system encourages new candidates to make extravagant charges against incumbents; the nature of candidate selection makes it likely for a new president to be unaware of the constraints on policy choices so that he or she makes empty promises that would be frightening if fulfilled and disillusioning if not.[1] Too often excesses of rhetoric and expectation overshadow quite sound policies. Although most Americans can make allowances for these peculiarities, foreigners cannot, and they find our policy process confusing and potentially dangerous as initiatives are often proclaimed, occasionally launched, and sometimes quickly countermanded. We compare very poorly with the Soviet Union in this aspect of the policy process, and, of course, the very openness of our society, when compared to Soviet society, underlies our inconsistency. Americans would not want to alter this situation; nevertheless, we should be able to do better—at least as well as other practicing democracies—in restoring some consensus about our foreign-policy strategy, in working out a set of broadly accepted tactics by which to implement that strategy, and in paying more attention to the consistency of our actions.

Consistency is not an end in itself; circumstances change and even the soundest approach sometimes fails and has to be altered. New priorities emerge; countering Soviet activities in the Horn of Africa, for example, overtook the need to reach arms-control arrangements for the Indian Ocean half way through the Carter administration. The perceived importance of regions changes: The Gulf became much more critical in the perceptions of many world leaders after the oil crises of the 1970s and its importance faded again as pressure on oil supplies abated. International interest in Africa has ridden a veritable roller coaster in the decades since its peoples achieved independence. In each of these cases, rigid consistency in policy would have been misplaced, but at the same time policy shifts were much more extreme than necessary. Third World policy is especially susceptible to seemingly capricious handling; we are less likely to take chances with our global concerns. When the two conflict, we tend to alter regional policies— sometimes very sharply—rather than rethink and change the global side of the equation.

There is little to suggest that the United States has plotted a course for dealing with the Third World, whether within administrations or between them. Our policymakers do not appear to weigh global and regional factors realistically, nor do they seem to have a clear, ultimate objective when they approach the Third World. If our policy is restoration of U.S. grandeur, it must be justified in terms of ends attainable in the real world. If it is a policy of devolution, it must set forth some other goal than avoiding unpleasant burdens. Our plans for the Third World deserve just as much attention as do our relations with our allies and principal adversaries.

We should not expect too much from the planning procedure. The world around us is ambiguous, and we have few opportunities to replicate past successes, such as the Marshall Plan. Even the best foreign-policy planning is less definitive than the proposals for, say, a manufacturing enterprise. At most the foreign-policy planner can control half the variables; the rest float freely in the outside world. However, even though foreign-policy planning is a very imperfect art, it is still an essential one; the United States must have a policy design and take advantage of circumstances that it cannot control, rather than be hostage to them.

Policymaking for the Third World suffers from one unique difficulty. Few senior U.S. officials, let alone members of the general public, have had experience dealing with Third World problems, except perhaps with those in the Middle East. Such problems are generally well understood only in academia and in the regionalist corners of such agencies as the Department of State and Central Intelligence Agency. The government organizes planning exercises on Third World issues and ensures that in crises balanced information will be available for decisionmakers. These individuals, however, will have difficulty accepting unfamiliar ideas that are incompatible with their globalist perspective and priorities and discordant with their outdated view of the world—one that almost invariably underestimates the salience of Third World issues and the competence of Third World governments. The only solution to this problem is to develop eduational systems that will expand the cognitive "maps" of future policymakers and make them more aware of Third World realities. In the short term, we must devise more effective bureaucratic mechanisms for providing information, for structuring choices in ways that emphasize regional considerations, and for focusing high-level attention on them.

The most important aid to forming policy is a framework within which decisionmakers and those who serve them can organize the facts they know, relate conflicting priorities, evaluate U.S. interests, gear rhetoric to reality, win support for policy, and develop plans that are consistent over the long term and have minimum aberrations over the short term. This policy concept will help senior officials to treat specific Third World problems in an intellectual context rather than to regard each one as an idiosyncratic event or merely as the outgrowth of global issues. It can also suggest to them ways in which to relate and balance global and regional concerns. On the basis of a broad strategy, they can better assess the wisdom of various courses of action.

Getting Americans to address issues in explicitly conceptual terms is no easy task. We take peculiar pride in our antitheoretical bent, and only a foreign-born American, Henry Kissinger, was able to impose some semblance of conceptual planning and action on the foreign-policy establishment. Concepts are not that frightening: In policymaking a conceptual approach amounts to little more than having some grasp of how the world is arranged and how we relate to it. Indeed, all people hold conceptions about the world and shape their actions accordingly. For instance the belief that the Third World is essentially backward and in need of step-by-step U.S. guidance and that the right-thinking citizens of Third World countries are eager for that guidance is a coherent concept. So is the related assumption that our global priorities should automatically take precedence over regional concerns because the latter are inherently less important. However, a serious problem arises because these attitudes are largely unstated and untested. Such attitudes must be examined in the daylight to see if they are really our beliefs and intentions and if they are valid when examined closely. If a concept is not stated by policymakers, it has little compelling power over those who are meant to implement it. The bureaucracy will either continue to follow its own agenda or make well-meant but often inept guesses about what the leadership wants.

A guiding concept is equlaly important to ensure that we do not take uninformed actions that will harm our objectives and interests. Many of the more egregious U.S. policy mistakes of the postwar years resulted not because policymakers had evil impulses or because there were no alternatives but because they were unaware of the available alternatives and of the potential effect of their actions. We will occasionally have to take actions that are distasteful or out of consonance with our long-term policy preferences. In making such a conscious decision, we should follow a process of considering whether a less harmful alternative may be available for meeting short-term requirements, deciding how and why we have diverged from our general course, and determining how we may offset the inevitable damage.

A Concept of Devolution

In addition to the paternalistic view of the Third World, there are a number of other possibilities, some of these are implicit in the strategy choices suggested in Chapter 5. Since the approach that I will apply in the remainder of this chapter will be the strategy of devolution, I will recapitulate the elements of the concept that I see underlying it.

1. Within the postimperial period of change the power positions of the United States, the Soviet Union, and the new Third World nations have shifted markedly. Our power is still great, but in relative terms it has declined significantly.

2. As Third World power has grown, a number of entities—states and subsystems—have increasingly demonstrated their ability to manage their own security. This process provides important opportunities for us to relinquish, more or less gradually, some of the security management burdens that we had assumed earlier, while still protecting our vital and important interests.

3. This process and our policy response to it can best be comprehended as a dialectical relationship between our global interests and responsibilities on the one hand and our regional interests and concerns on the other. Policy must be more attuned to the interactions of these

two spheres and, particularly, to the need for measured devolution of responsibility to Third World states and subsystems.

The first element is straightforward and hardly needs restatement. The data are incontrovertible and the implications reasonably unambiguous. However, few Americans have been able to adjust psychologically to a situation in which they are not militarily, economically, or even politically unique; they admit a slippage only in our position in the central balance against the Soviet Union. Despite Vietnam, Iran, and OPEC, growing Third World capabilities have simply not become a generally accepted proposition, and until they do we will be reacting to an unreal world.

The second element is more open to question, as we have seen in individual regions. Subsystems exhibit a wide range of capabilities, challenges, responses, and prospects, but even ASEAN, the most promising subsystem, does not have a secure future and is still politically and economically vulnerable. The GCC is even more vulnerable, SARC has barely begun to function, and both the Front Line and Contadora groups hold very tenuous prospects of permanence. Any of these subsystems could be dissolved in days by possible regional or global events. Certainly none would be capable of standing alone against a determined attack from its most likely enemy, whether the Soviet Union and its proxies or the Republic of South Africa.

The very existence of these groupings is, however, more remarkable than their weaknesses. A decade or so ago none of them existed, and few observers would have predicted this trend. Although the emergence of regional subsystems focused on security matters is not universal, it has occurred in widely different parts of the world because the phenomena that give rise to these groupings (the decline of imperialism and bipolarism) are global. Regional groupings appear to be developing somewhat at the expense of individual regional influentials, which might aspire to perform security management functions on their own. An India or a Nigeria could brush aside the constraints of a regional framework, but they would find it increasingly difficult to do so, just as another type of regional influential—such as Cuba or Iran—will find it increasingly hard to dominate a region from outside. South Africa has recently been able to advance its regional position at the cost of the Front Line states, but few would rate white South Africa's long-term leadership potential very high. The case of South Africa illustrates an important point: We are dealing with a broad, secular trend, and specific setbacks do not necessarily invalidate it as a focus for long-term policy analysis.

Also impressive, especially in comparison with the situation a decade or so ago, is the widespread realization that the first order of regional business is to settle the internal differences that provide the most promising opening for external intervention. ASEAN followed this approach, as has the GCC; in both cases the strongest regional member (Indonesia and Saudi Arabia, respectively) has made significant concessions by abandoning troublesome territorial claims. In South Asia, India under Rajiv Gandhi has only begun to attempt to improve regional relationships, and Pakistan's commitment to live at peace with a preeminent India has yet to be tested.

Despite regional variations the approach of regional grouping has shown considerable overall consistency: recognition of the undesirability and inefficacy of superpower interventions, generally purposeful action to reduce its likelihood, and measured confidence in their own ability to deal with nearby antagonists as long as these are not forcefully supported by a superpower patron. The nations involved have achieved a considerable level of maturity in their dealings with the international system. They have a sober view of the world around them and an intelligent approach to dealing with it.

The third element addresses the requirement for a conceptual framework to help the United States design Third World policies and mesh them with global priorities. The task of establishing a framework is particularly difficult because an unrelenting global perspective characterizes most Americans' thinking, even though its manifestations have been different during recent years. Kissinger's belief that the Soviet Union was the key problem in Angola was no more or less erroneous than the Carter administration's belief that nuclear nonproliferation was the key problem in our relationship with India. Although both assumptions contained some truth, the dogged U.S. pursuit of them to the exclusion of regional factors led, in the one case, to the increase of Soviet influence in Africa and, in the other, to the weakening of the nonproliferation regime as India prepared to scrap its entire nuclear agreement with us, including provisions for safeguards. Moreover, in both cases there was no shortage of regionalist advice to point out these possibilities.

The dispatch of the USS *Enterprise* on an apparently senseless mission into South Asian waters and, the entire policy tilt toward Pakistan in 1971 clearly illustrate how global priorities override regional considerations. Kissinger did not lack accurate information, and he fully understood the relative power relationships of the subcontinent. But his memoirs also illustrate how relatively unimportant such knowledge and understanding of the regional situation were for his policy choices. He based his decisions on global considerations regarding U.S. relations with China and the Soviet Union. South Asia as such was of little importance to the United States, and Kissinger rightly estimated that most of the broken crockery could be swept up later. If he were correct in his claim that his South Asian policies saved the world from a variety of disasters, the cost to South Asia and to the United States would have been a small price to pay.

The Central American policies of the Reagan administration, and even those of the last months of the Carter administration, were adopted despite the almost unanimous opinion of Latin American specialists who urged that the United States should rely heavily on the capabilities of the regional actors in the El Salvador crisis. The administration responded that U.S. vital interests are at stake in Central America and an image of resolve must be demonstrated to the global audience. The United States should not follow the regionalist approach, according to the administration, because the unproven abilities of other Caribbean countries are not adequate to guarantee U.S. interests. Needless to say, the administration's assumptions are not universally shared, just as Kissinger's were not in 1971 about South Asia.

Regionalist, devolutionary policies are no more entitled to automatic support than are globalist, interventionist ones. A policymaker does not need to be an unreconstructed globalist to be chary of adopting policies that further regional autonomy. We cannot assume that regional systems that have achieved autonomy will be able to guarantee our vital security interests in their own regions or that they will necessarily want to. And the U.S. security interests are vital in at least the Gulf region and in Central America. Although our interests are much less great in South Asia, we have substantial, if not vital, concerns in Southeast Asia and southern Africa.[2] Each of these situations must, however, be considered on its own merits and also in terms of the threat to our interests.

As we have seen, threats to our interests in the Third World come from two sources: from the Soviets and their proxies and from within an individual system. The Gulf is such a tremendous concern precisely because either variable could stop the flow of oil. The threat is much less great in Central America, since the United States could always reassert its interests against regional opposition and since there the Soviet Union would find it hard to mount threats significantly greater than those now posed by Cuba. In South Asia a Soviet threat from Afghanistan is more than potentially menacing, but it can probably be contained if India and Pakistan address it in a cooperative effort. The Cuban presence in southern Africa is not militarily decisive, and as long as China remains benevolent, Southeast Asia should not be exposed to any danger that it cannot handle with indirect U.S. backing. The dangers to U.S. interests from within these latter three systems do not appear serious unless we make exceptionally poor policy choices that alienate substantial parts of the system and perhaps drive them into a Soviet embrace.

Policymakers can conjure up more or less real visions of threats to important interests in any part of the world. The United States must always be concerned with the implications of being excluded anywhere in security terms, at least as long as it remains in global competition with the Soviet Union. Our case studies suggest that the kinds of legitimate access in which we are usually most interested probably would not be disturbed by regional autonomy. In most of the areas we are not impelled to seek hegemony. The Soviets in contrast appear to be driven in this direction, and in Asia particularly geography makes them a potential hegemonic power. Thus, when regions assert their autonomy, the Soviets are less likely to make the gains that might have fallen into their hands as we reduced the level of our involvement. In terms of U.S. interests and of the stability of the global system, the optimum situation would not be one of widespread U.S. dominance but one in which neither superpower was in a position, through influence or conquest, to deny the other's access to any subsystem.

Effective assertion of regional autonomy would be extremely useful in curbing the Soviet danger, but this approach would seem to involve an apparent, inherent disadvantage to our interests. The initial assertion of autonomy would usually be made at the cost of positions currently held by the United States and its allies; in only a few instances is a Third World country so close to the Soviet Union that Moscow would bear the heavier costs. This relative difference would be a problem only if the U.S.-Soviet competition in the Third World were a two-handed, zero-sum game in which all U.S. losses accrued to the Soviet Union as gains. Since this would be true only if we defined the situation in those terms, our "losses" will generally accrue to the region itself. Even then, the losses would be somewhat illusory because they would often include security involvements that entailed more costs than benefits. If a given country developed capabilities to defend itself, the United States would hardly need to bemoan the loss of our responsibility to defend it. When a country or region asked us to stay away, it would have to live with the consequences, and we could only assume that it had intelligently thought through the implications. We have, however, discovered a major exception to this proposition, arising from the interrelatedness of our global interests. Our involvement in Southeast Asia and in East and North Africa is not that important in protecting nations of the regions. U.S. presence, however, may be vital for projecting force and influence into the Gulf region and Middle East. In these cases we might have to override regional arguments concerning devolution and limitations of access. Before doing so, however, we want to look carefully at the costs and benefits involved.

Devolution of responsibility to the regional level can also have interesting implications for the global system, including the U.S.-Soviet rivalry. Although the rise of alternate sources of power will not displace bipolarity in the foreseeable future, it should attenuate that conflict as power is shared more widely and more cross-cutting interests deflect the superpowers from preoccupation with East-West affairs. Trends over the past decades have been generally, if erratically, in this direction, and that certainly was part of the theory behind nonalignment.

More speculatively, widespread assertion of autonomy could over time go far toward solving the Soviet Union's perceived parity deficiencies. Soviet protestations of a desire for parity may be little more than an attempt to mask a determination to achieve global domination. Parity would then be a sliding concept, and stability would be achieved only at the highest level of competition when the Soviets have realized that the United States cannot be outbid. Soviet policies and aspirations are not unalterable, however, and they may change as Moscow confronts increasingly discouraging realities. If there is some possibility of greater flexibility, U.S.-Soviet parity would be much better attained at a low rather than a high level. The Soviets complain that we and our allies are seemingly dominant in countries splashed all over the map, whereas their influence is limited mainly to geographically adjacent areas. If one accepts the Soviets' claim to superpower status, that is not an unreasonable complaint. To be sure, there is an easy answer: Improve your economic and political systems and you too can compete in nonmilitary ways. Like most easy answers, this answer does not get us very far, and the possibility of achieving a mutually satisfactory and reasonably stable parity at a low level, based on a policy of devolution, is not without interest. In most areas, a pullback of the United States from places that the Soviets (and ultimately the Chinese) see as provocatively near their borders could also contribute to stability, as would a Soviet withdrawal from Cuba.

At the same time, we must constantly recall the fact that global issues—especially our rivalry with the Soviet Union and the preservation of an international economic structure that protects our interests—are the ultimate concerns of U.S. policy. A purely regionalist perspective that fails to appreciate the global context could lead to uncoordinated policies and ultimate national disaster; regional policies must be pursued as part of an overall policy structure that strengthens our global position. We must establish the interrelationship between the two approaches and the validity of each. Global and regional elements will shift in importance according to time and place and call for some mixture.

That mixture needs to be informed by a grasp of history and a sense of overall direction, lest it become a collection of ad hoc responses to the conflicting pulls of the "old" global issues related to our competition with the Soviets, the "new" global issues of economic and world order concerns, and our regional interests.

For example, no policymakers doubt the need to contain the Soviet threat, but they must not make a priori assumptions about how that threat could be best contained when establishing policy for specific cases. Nobody doubts that nonproliferation is a desirable goal, but if the results of a country-by-country analysis show that the policy is repeatedly failing, then policymakers must rethink their overall strategy and readjust their estimate of attainable goals. No one would argue against a policy of maintaining good bilateral relations with the Philippines. However, the actual conduct of our relations there must not be based on vague ideas or romantic notions about the past; rather, it must come from a close analysis of whether we are paying too much, whether we are mortaging the future for the present, or whether global objectives (which are themselves in conflict) override bilateral and regional concerns.

Deciding the proportions of the policy mixture is ultimately just the sort of thing that presidents are elected to do. On the basis of the argumentation of this entire book, I hold that by accepting the first two elements—dealing with the nature of change in this country and in the postimperial world generally—we will interpret the third element in such a way that we will favor devolution of responsibility rather than U.S. assertiveness. The golden rule of subsidiarity underlies such an interpretation: Do not do things that others can do as well or at least well enough to prevent serious damage to your interests; and, concentrate on those things that you do well or uniquely. The remainder of this chapter suggests some of the things that the United States could do to move consistently in the direction of devolution while still protecting itself against threats that could not be handled by regional forces.[3]

Doing Well What We Do Best

The actions uniquely within the province of the United States—or at most shared with a few other great powers—relate to the global order. Preeminent among these is the maintenance of the strategic balance and the related responsibility of preventing war, especially nuclear war, between the superpowers. Obviously, a superpower war could inflict intolerable harm on the Third World as well as on the First and Second, whether through global fallout and nuclear winter or by extreme disruption of the interdependent world economy. However, we hardly need this worry to increase our determination not to destroy ourselves.

More relevant, the U.S.-Soviet balance is vital to Third World countries because it permits them considerable freedom of political action. Even such a major power as India would find its nonalignment meaningless if the United States (or the Soviet Union) abandoned a global role or became so weak that it no longer posed a credible deterrent to its rival. Our concern is not solely the result of solicitude for Third World diplomacy; it is very much in our interest that Third World countries—not to mention China—retain sufficient freedom of political maneuver to prevent the Soviet Union from extending its hegemony.

As we have noted, awareness that a capable and well-disposed superpower is nearby to limit disruptive intrusions from other outside sources was a necessity in forming regional systems in Western Europe and Southeast Asia. Contadora and SARC could not enjoy their current freedom of action if the United States did not counterbalance Cuba and the Soviet Union; and our background role in the Gulf is even more critical. The latter role entails more than U.S. capability to fight a nuclear war; to be credible it must also include the ability to (1) project conventional forces into regions that lack the indigenous strength to hold off Soviet pressures and (2) deny access to the Soviet Union or its proxies should they seek to impose their political will or to prop up tottering, friendly regimes. These roles could be played either by the United States directly or by U.S. allies who know that they can rely on effective U.S. support if they run into trouble with the Soviets. (French assistance to several African states is a case in point.)

Our strategic capabilities are determined by considerations that bear little direct relationship to Third World concerns; a balance acceptable by other criteria would also meet these. Conventional projection forces—rapid deployment forces, naval and air transport, part of our carrier fleet—are justifiable primarily in terms of Third World contingencies. As we saw in the case studies, most subsystems see at least a potential Soviet threat. They are concerned about a counterbalancing U.S. strategic capability and also want the United States to maintain tactical capabilities that would be available locally when needed. There is little enthusiasm anywhere for a visible and permanent U.S. presence. Although several Central American countries seek direct U.S. involvement, that position is not held by the Contadora Group or by Latin Americans in general. In South Asia, Pakistan has disclaimed any readiness to host U.S. forces, and India leads the campaign to evict us from Diego Garcia. The fragile Gulf states, Oman aside, want U.S. support to be available but discreetly over the horizon. The issue of a U.S. military presence does not arise in southern Africa, and ASEAN's enthusiasm for the U.S. presence in the Philippines is closely related to the Soviet naval presence in Vietnam.

The regional states' concern about the Soviet danger is considerably less in most cases than their preoccupation with a well-defined threat posed by a local regional power (Vietnam, Cuba, South Africa, or Israel). To the extent that Cuba and Vietnam are perceived as Soviet proxies, of course, the distinction may be without much difference.

Such diverse and vague concerns do not translate readily into U.S. force levels, and specifics in this area are not within my competence. The logic of the presentation, however, does suggest some broad requirements. The size, composition, mission, and basing of forces dedicated to Third World contingencies should be thought of in "sunset" terms and should not take on a momentum of their own. The role of U.S. military support is to protect and hearten regional forces so that the latter can increasingly assume regional security responsibility within the context of the U.S.-Soviet balance. Although in some cases this arrangement may never be attained, it should be a goal whenever possible. For example, it would be senseless to abandon the Philippine bases by supporting the theoretical proposition that ASEAN should stand on its own. At the same time, however, our military planning should take active account of a longer term contingency under which ASEAN would grow in capability, reach some modus vivendi with Vietnam, and propose withdrawal of both Soviet and U.S. bases from the region. If this option is attractive to us, it should not be precluded by the need to remain in Clark Field and Subic Bay because of their importance for other U.S. global considerations or because our military lacks flexibility. Similarly, our military activities in Central America should be designed to facilitate the transfer of responsibility to regional forces rather than to perpetuate a U.S. presence. U.S. military forces designated for Third World missions are the instrument of policy—in this case a policy of devolution—and must not become an impediment to that policy.

Military forces should be structured in ways that maximize an over-the-horizon capability. Actual positioning of U.S. military forces in places such as Pakistan or the Gulf could draw us into commitments and regional quarrels that we would rather avoid and would probably retard the development of indigenous security management capabilities. Although maintaining such a posture is certainly more difficult and in some cases impossible in the near term, it should be a clearly understood objective. Our regional survey has clearly shown one thing: the irrelevance of applied U.S. military force to most of the pressing problems we and our friends are facing. The purpose of U.S. military capability is to provide a political context rather than to fight battles. Even though the capability to do the latter is essential to the former, the basic priority must always be at the center of our planning.

The United States bears another kind of global responsibility of crucial importance—providing an economic environment that enables Third World nations to pursue their legitimate interests in development and to maintain an economic base consistent with internal and external security demands. We share responsibilities in the economic area with the Europeans, the Japanese, and even the Soviets who must bear an amount proportionate to their capabilities. The largest share is ours, however, for we have the greatest capabilities and have been the principal organizer of the system.

We and our allies must maintain healthy and open economies that can provide capital, technology, trade, and investment for the Third World. These economies will form part of a viable international system, whether based on Bretton Woods or not, within which all countries can pursue their legitimate interests. This much is simple and obvious self-interest. Beyond that is a moral imperative to provide economic assistance that most Americans recognize but have never found satisfactory ways of expressing. Less obvious is the necessity to develop policies responsive to the needs of individual Third World countries and to the larger North-South agenda, which is stated largely in economic terms. An extensive literature is devoted to this subject, and some of the ideas characterized as neorealism seem to make good sense.[4] In the long run, reasonable economic aspirations of the South will have to be accommodated if we are to live in a minimally comfortable world. This thought takes on a disturbing dimension when we project some trends that we discussed earlier, for we have yet to encounter economic demands backed up by military muscle.

Despite the seeming salience of economic factors, we err when we put them at the head of the North-South agenda. The contest is a political one for control of the international economic system as a whole rather than for specific reforms or potential benefits. The inscription on Kwame Nkrumah's statue, "Seek first the political kingdom," is understood beyond the borders of Ghana to mean that the transfer of economic power will come only as part of a transfer of political power. Also noteworthy is how small a role economics plays in the formation of regional systems. ASEAN used economic cooperation as a stepping stone, and SARC is following that lead: In both bases, however, the primary motivation for cooperation was political.

Dealings between almost any two nations routinely have extensive economic content, but even for nations with interdependent economies, economics is rarely at the core of their relationship. This is also true for U.S. dealings with Third World countries except perhaps with those that are so weak that they have no significant political ambitions. Our relationship with the more important Third World countries focuses heavily on security and political matters, and our attempts to divert these into an economic framework are seldom successful. Aid programs, trade concessions, and even technology transfers are rarely so important that they produce concessions on matters of political significance to the recipient country. Given the choice between military assistance or special political recognition, on one hand, and economic benefits realistically within U.S. capabilities, on the other, most important Third World countries would opt for the former. When we assume that achievable economic programs would extinguish southern protest, we miss the whole point: We do not have the resources that would be required, and the emerging nations are concerned with the effective transfer of power in the postimperial period.

Despite their growing strength, developing countries are far from holding the kind of political power that would compel a sharp reordering of the present global economic structure. Our ultimate interests might best be served by reordering that structure in ways compatible with the desires of these developing nations; it would almost certainly be in our interest to make major concessions to some regional groupings and some individual states, either because of their economic importance to us or as a means of strengthening them to exercise their regional capabilities more effectively. The Gulf states, India, ASEAN, and perhaps Mexico are in this category. There is no obvious reason, however, for us to strengthen such southern forums as the Group of 77. The interests of such groups and those of the United States range from mildly compatible to unreconcilable in both economic and political spheres, and it is not readily evident that they are engaged in any activity that contributes to the kind of global system that would best serve our interests. When we agree to negotiate on such broad matters as the Common Fund for commodities, we would do well to think of them in political rather than economic terms. For the most part we are better advised to deal in smaller forums, which are at least partially defined by us, and to focus on taking action that may economically benefit the recipient.

Bilateral economic assistance is an important exception to this approach. Although sometimes desirable in promoting specific U.S. interests or targeting assistance very precisely, bilateral aid relationships are generally not politically appropriate in dealings with nations preoccupied with their sovereignty and nationalism. Client relationships were suitable in the imperial era, but they are inappropriate in one in which we encourage Third World nations to assert their autonomy. In addition, bilateral aid relationships risk drawing us into political situations of little interest to us. Resource transfer is needed on economic and especially moral grounds.[5] The preferred vehicle should be the international lending institutions, and our commitments there should be very generous because we have a strong interest in involving Third World countries in a functioning international economy. Generous contributions will also help ensure that these institutions will operate in ways compatible with U.S. interests.

Some intriguing middle ground can be found between the global and bilateral economic approaches. Expectations that regional economic projects, such as Mekong Valley development, would reduce regional conflict were ill founded, but economic policies that reinforce regional groupings could make sense. By dealing with ASEAN and the EC as units, we have strengthened their ability to turn to sensitive security and political matters with greater confidence. A Caribbean Basin initiative that seeks to preempt the regional political process will fail; one that supports a viable process could be indispensable. Should India and its neighbors get together on regional projects such as joint river development, it is in our interests to see that their plans have sufficient financial backing to keep them constructively engaged. If the black states of southern Africa could strengthen themselves economically, and if we could provide incentives to further cooperation, the future of that region would probably weigh less heavily on us.

Finally, there is the question of South-South cooperation. It would be undesirable for this to entail a split of the global economic system or substantial redirection of international trade. In fact, though, such grandiose results can hardly be expected, and South-South cooperation is likely to flourish much more on a local level. This could be beneficial to the formation and strengthening of regional subsystems or to the peaceful coexistence and cooperation of adjacent systems such as South Asia and the Gulf.

What we do best as a nation emphatically includes taking care of our own interests. For better or worse, that is the essence of the nation-state—and nobody else is going to do it for us. As a superpower with global leadership responsibilities, the United States owes it to itself to maintain those interests, but it also owes it to the well-being of the global order that, without a strong United States, would be worse off than it is now. This is not ethnocentrism or an assertion that we play our role as effectively and justly as we should but a statement of obvious fact. The U.S. presence is as critical a factor in global security as a strong U.S. economy is essential to global economic development. We cannot simply assume that all regional trends are moving in stately progress toward desirable goals. Many Americans would argue that the rise even of effective regionalism in Central America or the Gulf cannot be an acceptable alternative to U.S. primacy since in such areas we must be in a position to ward off threats to our vital interests. The fact that this argument is the same one that some Soviets make about Eastern Europe and Afghanistan renders it no more or less valid.

Something that we alone can do—but often do not do very well—is come to terms with the ambivalence of our own power. We no longer control the bulk of relevant (nonnuclear) power in the world, especially as it pertains to Third World issues. We can no longer assume that we have the capability to ensure access—or even in all cases to confidently protect our vital interests. We cannot guarantee that oil will flow from Gulf wells at reasonable prices nor ensure collection of debts owed to our banks. As we learned in Vietnam, we cannot ensure favorable outcomes even in security matters. We no longer have the overabundant resources and power that allowed overinsurance against all contingencies and a seemingly infinite margin for error. We have learned much about the limitations of power in the later years of the twentieth century.

As we look at individual regions, China and even Japan rival us in Southeast Asia; the Soviets have a stronger position in South Asia and maintain a brooding presence in the Gulf and Middle East; and the French are more effective in much of Africa. Only in Central America does the United States have the capability to manage regional security; elsewhere it would entail great effort or even a redefinition of our national purpose.

At the same time, however, U.S. global power remains unequaled, and with a major effort it could prevail in most parts of the world. We continue to have a very large, if diminished, margin for error and to maintain a great degree of flexibility. What would be a vital blow to the interest of almost any other state is often for us only an inconvenience worth risking in our pursuit of larger goals.

We can draw two points from this ambivalent situation. First, even when we have limited power to achieve positive ends, such as promoting devolution with individual systems, our negative power remains decisive. We can frustrate the development of systems simply by playing super-power politics and committing a modest amount of military support to our chosen instrument. This combination of strengths and weaknesses can make us extremely dangerous—able to destroy but not rebuild, frustrate but not induce. It enjoins upon us the duty of being extremely cautious and thoughtful in our actions.

Second, we need to recast our thinking—in part at least—away from the idea of power to that of influence. Even when our power is absent or irrelevant, we are regarded as a potential helpful hand in strengthening regional security, we remain an almost indispensable party to any critical international event, we play a predominant economic role, and our own culture penetrates to the unlikeliest corners of the earth. Although some Third World nations would like to see our power reduced, almost all welcome a substantial degree of U.S. influence and believe that they can harness it to their benefit. Influence in this sense is closely related to what was defined in earlier chapters as the legitimate access that we require. This influence will not guarantee protection of all our interests as unlimited power might, but it does provide a critical margin for the policymaker with nerves strong enough to use it.

Letting Others Do What They Do Best

Doing well the things that we do best is only half a policy. The other half involves dealing with Third World nations and subsystems in ways that permit them to do what they do best—cope with their own problems on their own terms. This means scaling down our demands and expectations. The most that we can reasonably hope for is that the interests of regional influentials and regional systems will generally run parallel to our own in developing autonomy and preserving the kinds of access that we require. This approach means that we must rely on influence more than on power to achieve our ends. If we are forced to utilize power to gain a higher level of access into a subsystem's security affairs, we will breach the ability of that subsystem to do the things it should do on its own. Such intrusions must be kept to a minimum and must be regarded as measures of last resort.

We also cannot expect that these nations will be either proxies or allies; we will share no identity of interests with them. Our relationship may involve little more than the absence of conflict. This bond may not seem very great, especially for an America that has universal aspirations for its values and its system, but we cannot realistically expect such vastly different nations to share with us a broad range of security or economic interests.

No grouping looks to the United States for regional leadership, and only ASEAN comes fairly close to assuming that its interests generally coincide with ours. At the other extreme, we are a major element of the problem in Central America because of our capability to play a hegemonic role and because of the largely negative image that our previous actions have earned us there. Some groups see the United States as a potential threat (or at least an element of disturbance), but nowhere are we regarded with equanimity nor should we expect to be, in view of our immense power and global involvements. The late Wayne Wilcox aptly described our image as that of a "generally benign elephant interested in a stable jungle but on occasion given to careless romps."[6]

If the countries of the Third World do not see the United States as much more of a natural ally than they do the Soviet Union, they nevertheless believe that we are capable of doing more things for them—

one of the measures of influence. If we are adroit, we may also cause them fewer problems, although the very complexity of our web of relationships means that there will be many points of conflict as well as cooperation. This position may be quite enough to secure our vital and important interests and is probably about all the traffic will bear. It also leaves open the possibility—albeit not one that we should bank on—for developing a closer identity of interests and values over time.

We should encourage the emergence of states and systems that represent intrinsic strength and see their interests as broadly parallel (or at least not in opposition) to our own. In earlier days we could choose freely among possible Third World associates, but we no longer have that luxury. Regional circumstances, not U.S. manipulation, will produce the regional security managers of the future. This situation might at times force us to swallow some unpleasant realities, for example, if, hypothetically, Nigeria should decide to take a firm hand in shaping up its neighbors. Unless we are willing to expend the resources to manage regional security ourselves, however, we have few alternatives, and there is no reason to assume that we would be able to do a more just job.

A related item of self-restraint suggests that even while we support regionally significant nations and groupings, we should maintain some distance from those whom we favor. It is not in our interest for nations to assume that we would automatically support them any more than that we would automatically oppose them. By making them look like clever children whom we are anxious to adopt, we risk giving the kiss of death. They will reach maturity in response to their own requirements, and they will pursue policies that suit them. We can do little to alter those policies and still less in creating them.

One of the most difficult tests of U.S. nerves has been violent revolutionary change in Third World regions in which we have significant interests and a comfortable relationship with the incumbent regimes. Change of this type is a main characteristic of Third World societies, and the United States can do little to forestall it. Even when change is revolutionary, the outcome will usually provide us with sufficient access to ensure our interests. Of course, many of the fundamental changes in the Third World are long overdue. Although short-term manifestations are often difficult to deal with without institutions for peaceful change, our interests and these of the people involved might be better served in the long term by revolution. When instability is not likely to deprive us of necessary access and does not have a significant negative impact on the global balance (in other words, the instability would not cause an important country to align itself irrevocably with the Soviet Union), we can generally stand back and let the chips fall where they may. Our best protection is to promote the view among newly emerging leaders—perhaps several rapidly changing generations of them—that the United States is not threatening their interests and can help maintain a balance against possible Soviet assertiveness. Managing to ensure such a future for the United States, while still maintaining high levels of access in important areas ruled by regimes ripe for revolution, has been a principal dilemma for U.S. tacticians in dealing with the Third World, and there is no simple solution to it, whether in Iran, Nicaragua, or the Philippines. The more we can limit our need for access in prerevolutionary situations (very difficult) and identify such situations (much easier), the better is our chance of surviving the revolutionary fallout.

Strong nerves are not necessarily accompanied by an absence of concern, and we have a responsibility to respond to requests for assistance from responsible nations faced with a direct and credible threat, especially one from the Soviet Union. If the United States alone can provide such assistance and it is necessary, useful, and feasible, it must be accepted as part of our superpower responsibilities. Requests for assistance should be scrutinized closely because in more cases than one might expect local forces can deal with even Soviet intrusions not involving military force. The most difficult cases are indirect aggression and externally supported subversion, the middle ground between clear domestic unrest and direct external aggression. No automatic guidelines can be established, but when Soviet involvement is indirect and not decisive, we should stand aside lest we raise the stakes and trigger a still larger Soviet role.

The Reagan Doctrine will have to be subjected to this kind of analysis. Not every group proclaiming itself to be anti-Soviet is an appropriate object of U.S. assistance. Two basic tests might be these: (1) Is the resistance group self-generated and inherently strong, rather than a creature of U.S. policy? (2) Is it supported by a regional consensus, so that we can expect at least substantial moral support for ourselves and our client? The Kampuchean and Afghan resistance forces clearly meet both these criteria and, perhaps not coincidentally, also enjoy widespread support within the United States. The UNITA forces in Angola readily meet the first criterion but because of their ties to South Africa have little support from other nations in the region. It would be difficult to make a convincing case for the Nicaraguan Contras on either count.

The United States might also serve its own interests by providing assistance in contingencies where the Soviets are not involved because it has many other interests in the Third World besides simply countering the Soviet Union. We should limit outselves to supplementing the strength of healthy systems (such as ASEAN) rather than engaging in fruitlessly compensating for the inherent weaknesses of such systems as the old

SEATO or a would-be ally that shows small promise of viability. Nations usually seek commitments from us when they are losing a regional contest, and it rarely serves our interest to aid them at this point. Commitments consume our resources, they may retard the natural processes of system building, and they often make it difficult for us to contrbute to long-term, stable outcomes. The commitments that the United States does make should be limited, clearly defined, and designed to restrain our partners from either drawing us into quarrels outside our sphere of interest or acting irresponsibly from underneath our protective umbrella. Our relationship with Somalia presented special challenges in this regard, and we seem to have met them well so far; the most striking negative example is the relationship we entered into with Pakistan in the 1950s. When we take on unsupportable commitments, we expose the other party to unfair risk—something neither politically nor morally acceptable.

On any count, the key injunction for the United Sates is "first of all, do no harm." This advice is not heroic, especially when compared to earlier slogans, such as "bear any burden," but it does seem appropriate now that our resources are in short supply and other nations are increasingly able to assume their own burdens.

There remains the question of when direct U.S. intervention is an appropriate and necessary deviation from a policy of support for regional autonomy. There is no general answer, but a decision to intervene, made necessary by intelligently perceived national interest or by concern for long-term regional development, should be reached only after the regional alternative has gotten a fair hearing. Because of the predominant global perspective of U.S. policymakers the burden of proof now tends to rest on the regionalists, who must demonstrate that their solutions are preferable. The primary burden of proof should now be shifted onto those who urge global approaches to Third World situations. When a globalist approach is proposed that could lead to significant intervention by the United States, its supporters should have to demonstrate

1. That the U.S. interest involved is of an exceptionally high level, probably vital to our national security and well-being.
2. That there is a clear and present threat to this interest that cannot be dealt with by less interventionist means, including by using the capabilities of regional powers.
3. That U.S. involvement is going to be effective or that even a failed attempt is clearly preferable to inactivity.[7]

Not many situations exist in which these three criteria can be intelligently and honestly judged as present. When they are and we intervene, an integral part of the planning process should be devoted to seeing how our involvement can be shaped to restore and enhance the autonomy of the nation or system. The resulting policy may include a rapid disassociation from a weak client that we have been propping up or a strengthening of the most likely claimant to our leadership role. Intervention in regional affairs buys time; if we fail to use that time wisely, our actions will have been meaningless.

Regional Applications

This book provides no precise guidance on how to answer difficult questions such as those posed at the end of Chapter 6; in the last analysis each individual will have to make choices in concrete situations and under conflicting circumstances that do not admit to much useful generalization. There is, therefore, little point in prescribing region-specific strategies. It will be useful, however, to look again very briefly at some of the courses of action that could be followed in relating concept to reality. Only a few particularly salient issues will be raised; playing out all the options against all issues in all regions would be tedious and not very informative (although this is precisely the course of a full-scale policy planning exercise within the government).

Beginning with Southeast Asia, the range of available short-term choices is very narrow and will probably remain so until the United States and the Soviet Union move away from a rigid cold-war posture and until more flexible approaches are used for dealing with the Third World. (This is true for other regions as well.) In the not too distant future, however, the United States may find itself facing some basic decisions about the future of its relationships in Southeast Asia. The first policy reevaluation would concern Vietnam, if Hanoi is able to reach some agreement with the ASEAN nations. Our global anti-Communist posture, reinforced by Sino-Vietnamese enmity, may push us toward continued hostility with Vietnam even if ASEAN were to ask us to be more open as an aid in socializing Vietnam or even exploiting Hanoi's restiveness over its heavy deepndence on the Soviet Union.

Another potential problem is restriction of U.S. military access in the Philippines. Would the United States, in this case, be willing to allow ASEAN to determine the response or would unilateral and global concerns override regional considerations? Most difficult would be the dilemma posed earlier: If ASEAN should succeed in establishing a Zone of Peace, Freedom and Neutrality that was in other respects satisfactory to us, would we be willing or able to move out of the Philippine bases as part of the package?

Alternately, if the United States were able to consolidate its relations with China and Japan, would our global interests be served by inducing ASEAN to join in a Pacific Security Community directed against the Soviet Union and Vietnam? In still another dimension, can we envision a future in which China played a more independent, perhaps menacing role toward Southeast Asia and in which a Soviet presence could usefully contribute to a regional balance of power supported from the outside?

These contingencies are not of immediate concern; one's preference among them will depend on an estimate of the future U.S. role in the world, the potential of the ASEAN countries, the long-term outlook for Soviet policy, and an estimate of how Chinese policy will evolve.

A policy of devolution would emphasize regional autonomy in Southeast Asia, based on the assumption that U.S. interests there are not vital. It would emphasize a U.S. participation in a power balance orchestrated by ASEAN rather than the inclusion of ASEAN in a U.S.-led security consensus embracing all East Asia, which would perpetuate the region's role on a major fault line of the East-West confrontation. Inherent in this strategy is a preference for drawing Vietnam into a Southeast Asian system rather than perpetuating its role as an expensive Soviet client or supporting Chinese pressures on Vietnam. The United States would be seeking to exclude the Soviets (and perhaps itself) from security management in Southeast Asia, rather than containing or balancing the Soviets on the ground. Ultimately we would be supporting ASEAN's preference for an external power balance based upon the absence of the United States and the Soviet Union, rather than upon regional competition between them.

For the most part our regional policies are compatible with this strategy: we have, for instance, wisely acceded to ASEAN's request that we supply assistance to the Kampuchean resistance. Yet it is not clear whether the U.S. government has this approach in mind as its long-term goal or, indeed, whether it has thought the matter through at a sufficiently high level. If such consideration has not been given, then the United States may face some very tough choices in the not too distant future and may lack the guideline by which to shape its reactions. Without a concept of the future, the pressures to accommodate global pressures—especially the need to maintain the Philippine bases for Gulf contingencies and the potential need to placate China—could rapidly undo what has been accomplished.

Aside from thoughtful planning, a devolution policy calls for U.S.-ASEAN consultation on long-term strategy; for conversations with the Japanese and Chinese to avoid surprising them by an unexpected U.S. response to situations that might develop quickly; for avoidance of rhetoric that asserts vital U.S. interests in Southeast Asia and its sea-lanes or exaggerates the threat; and for firm but quiet political support for ASEAN. The United States would allow ASEAN to set the pace in relations with Vietnam as regards both Kampuchea and diplomatic relations with Hanoi, on the assumption that ASEAN's stake in Vietnam is larger than the U.S. or Chinese stake and that integration of this regional deviant into the Southeast Asian system is very important. Since this tack would have negative domestic repercussions, we should start early to explain our position to concerned domestic audiences, such as relatives of U.S. military personnel still missing in Indochina.

The United States would follow a two-track security policy. We would show a steadiness in our commitment to the region and such demonstrations of our capabilities as we and ASEAN would find mutually useful. We would emphasize that our presence in the Philippines is a response to Southeast Asian requirements, and we would take some initial steps enabling us to withdraw from the Philippines should ZOPFAN become a reality. A short-term bonus of the deglobalization of the Philippine bases would be to decrease Manila's bargaining power and perhaps reduce political pressures on the fledgling democratic regime.[8]

Let me emphasize that this list of steps is only illustrative, not comprehensive, and many variations would be compatible with progress toward devolution. It does, however, point up that U.S. policymakers have moves to make, moves that will not cause major problems for U.S. policies and posture in Asia. Hard decisions may have to be made in the future; we will be able to make them with greater confidence if we have planned for them.

We have already seen our role diminish in South Asia; current choices center on whether we want to try to recoup part of it in light of our new Gulf concerns and the Soviet thrust into Afghanistan. An attempt to involve South Asia in U.S. Gulf policy, however, risks reinforcing polarization in South Asia that would draw India closer to the Soviet Union and thereby undercut our position in South Asia, perhaps resulting in a greater threat to Pakistan than if it were left to its own devices.

The beginning of wisdom in South Asia is recognition that the United States cannot organize the region's security. Even if only India opposed us it would be a herculean effort on our part to bring preponderant force to bear there. Since India could and would turn to the Soviet Union, which is much closer to South Asia than is the United States and which has a much greater stake, the task is nearly hopeless. Even the addition of China to a Washington-Islamabad entente would not tip the balance. The United States can gain no conceivable advantage by pushing South Asia into the East-West context, as long as India remains a predominant regional power and has access to Soviet support. Forcing India into a definitive commitment to the Soviet Union would be extremely costly and outweigh virtually anything else that might be gained in the process.

Although less self-evident, Pakistan cannot be separated from the South Asian system, as desirable as that might seem to us, the Pakistanis, and even many Indians. Pakistan cannot be a negligible factor in any power equation, and the historic Indo-Pakistani conflict has been so sharp, that India cannot ignore Pakistan as a factor in South Asian politics.

Reconciliation between India and Pakistan is critical to almost any U.S. strategy in Asia. If we had to move closer to Pakistan, it would be much less costly if the two subcontinental nations were on good terms and India did not feel threatened by U.S.-Pakistani ties. For a policy of devolution, Indo-Pakistani rapprochement is indispensable. In either case, ability of the two to cooperate on South Asian security matters would relieve the United States of responsibility toward South Asia except for maintaining the U.S.-Soviet strategic balance. During the early 1980s, Indo-Pakistani relations have frequently been strained, and especially since 1983, earlier progress has been largely lost. With the change in government in India, the potential for rapprochement is renewed but with no guarantee of success. We can do little to promote improved relations—much less even than we can in Southeast Asia—but certainly we must do what we can as a matter of top priority. The SARC framework shows promise as a vessel within which Indo-Pakistani hostility can be contained, but effusive U.S. support for it would be counterproductive. Should SARC request support from us or from the international lending institutions (e.g., for development of the Ganges and Brahmaputra river systems), we should be supportive as a means of strengthening and providing incentives for regional cooperation.

The more immediate U.S. concern should be avoiding actions that could undermine regional cooperation and especially Indo-Pakistani rapprochement. Our rhetoric has been in the right direction and the Reagan administration has shown a genuine desire to keep lines open to India, but in our actions we have sometimes wandered onto other tangents. This critical element needs to be accorded top priority in our South Asian policy planning and in our deliberations with both India and Pakistan. Our relationship with China also impacts on the region. Although South Asian matters cannot dictate our ties with Beijing, we may want to adjust them just as we will want to modify some of our support of China in consideration of ASEAN's preferences. Such adjustments would be much easier to make if we consulted frequently with China about our mutual stakes in the region, a subject on which the Chinese have shown considerable flexibility.

U.S. relations with India, the regionally dominant power, need careful tending. Since we cannot compete directly with the Soviet Union in the areas of its strength vis-à-vis India, we need to make maximum use of our own strengths in the economic area. Aside from special attention to bilateral economic issues such as trade and technology transfer, we should review our policies on Indian access to the international lending institutions. In the past several years we have taken actions adverse to India in the International Monetary Fund and Asian Development Bank. Although these moves were sensible in terms of our global economic criteria, we should look more closely at adapting these criteria to regional priorities when cases arise regarding India or other nations of special concern.

These self-evident regional policies are, however, held hostage by concerns arising outside the region—East-West tensions and U.S. interests in the Gulf—that render it highly problematic whether we can pursue our regional interests. If we must draw much closer to Pakistan and thus almost inevitably intensify the East-West overlay on the Indo-Pakistani dispute, the price will be very high and we must be certain it is worth it. Should further deterioration occur in the Gulf (for instance, an entrenchment of Soviet power in Iran) that forced us into complete alliance with Pakistan, we must be prepared to write off India and probably the rest of South Asia as the price of our global requirements and then do what we could—if possible with Chinese support—to guarantee Pakistan's security in the face of a hostile Indo-Soviet alliance. This is, however, a counsel of desperation, in the interest of no country except the Soviet Union. Both India and Pakistan realize that such a polarization would be disastrous for themselves and want to preserve their autonomy; these realizations give the United States a foundation upon which to build a devolution policy compatible with its interests. India and Pakistan already play significant and useful roles in the Gulf region, and if they could bridge their differences, their cooperative approach to the region would do much to offset the Soviet threat. To the extent that we are able to reduce our dependence and that of our allies on oil from the Gulf, our need to be involved with Pakistan will be less pressing, but this consideration far transcends our South Asian concerns. In any case, Pakistan is hardly indispensable in our Gulf strategy, and it is likely to play a role parallel to our own in any contingency short of U.S.-Arab hostilities (in which Pakistan would not support us in any case). The United States should resolutely resist the temptation to establish military facilities or bases in South Asia that would perpetuate polarization, prevent Indo-Pakistani cooperation, and identify the United States too closely with a regime in Pakistan that has still to establish its legitimacy.

Another global consideration is the role of South Asia in East-West matters. Here, again, it seems self-evident that the United States should do all it can to minimize the overlay of the two rivalries. India is not likely to become an adjunct to Soviet policy unless we force it to. Arming Pakistan against the Soviet threat is sensible only up to a point; beyond that its security is weakened in the face of Indian fears. We need to define that point much more clearly in our own minds and in our dealings with Pakistan. Does it make sense, for instance, to supply Pakistan with weapons systems virtually irrelevant to any threat except from India? (The Harpoon antiship missiles are the most striking example.) Thus far the Indians have found the level of U.S. support to Pakistan tolerable, if objectionable. We cannot give New Delhi any veto right over our relations with others; the realities of South Asia suggest, however, that we should take Indian concerns into account and consult with New Delhi.

The other East-West issue is the situation in Afghanistan. It is regrettable that Afghanistan became an East-West issue rather than remaining where it belongs—a matter of East-South contention. If the United States is unable to restore it to that context, the obvious step is for us to promote a settlement that removes Soviet presence from Afghanistan, even though this step would mean lessening pressure on the Soviets and might actually increase Soviet influence in Afghanistan above the level enjoyed before 1978.

In South Asia itself, applying the equation of threats and interests produces so low a level of interest that U.S. intervention or even intrusion simply cannot be justified. Because of the nature of the system even actions not intended to be intrusive can do major harm to regional moves toward autonomy. Regrettably, the United States cannot restore the 1977 situation in which it could stand completely aside from South Asian security affairs. U.S. involvement, however, must be shaped by the understanding that our goal is not only a South Asia that is secure and autonomous but also one that can play a positive role in nearby areas of greater intrinsic interest, especially the Gulf, rather than one that is hostage to our regional and global policies.

As we have seen, the Arab-Israeli conflict, its repercussions within the core area of the Middle East, and the involvement of the United States and the Soviet Union make the region a particularly unpromising one in which to implement a policy of devolution, or a policy of condominium with the Soviet Union. There is no shortage of prescriptions for dealing with the continuing Middle East crisis, and this study has not uncovered striking new ideas or approaches. Since the Middle East cannot be exempted from the dictates of rational policymaking, however, I will make some brief observations that follow from the general approach we have been pursuing.

First, the strong link between global and regional security concerns in the core of the Middle East does not mean that sharp East-West polarization is a happy situation, much less a desirable goal. Nowhere else in the Third World have the superpowers come so close to direct confrontation; as much maneuvering room as possible should be introduced for safety purposes. Although this linkage has undermined the autonomy of the region and its members, the superpowers have also lost much of their autonomy and have been drawn into courses of action that are more in the interests of the regional allies than of the superpowers themselves. Although the United States successfully kept its lines open to most of the Arab states, even greater freedom of action would be desirable. As Robert Neumann has pointed out, when we treat Syria in an East-West framework, we drive it closer to the Soviet Union and our prophecy becomes self-fulfilling.[9] Certainly a total polarization that left the United States standing alone with Israel would entail huge political costs within the Middle East and in the world.

Second, the Middle East is not exempt from the trends we have seen elsewhere in the international system. Military capabilities in the region have grown enormously; this growth, coupled with the individual states' abilities to manipulate superpower patrons, has drastically reduced the ability of the United States—or any outside power—to manage the security of the region. Syria successfully faced down the United States in Lebanon, and Iraq resisted Soviet pressures connected with the Iran-Iraq war. Given the decline in our managerial capabilities, the United States should resist becoming drawn into regional affairs unless a matter of real importance ot the East-West relationship or other U.S. national interests are at stake. It is difficult to see, for instance, how the recent U.S. involvement in Lebanon met either of these criteria, and we would not have become involved if the costs had been foreseen. Although it may be unfair to fault the United States for not foreseeing those consequences, we may ask whether the initial involvement—no matter how well intended—was a responsibility that this country needed to undertake.

Third, we should develop a policy concept and compatible policy goals, if we are going to make intelligent judgments about where our interests lie and which involvements are necessary and which can be avoided. Undeniably, a settlement of the Arab-Israeli problem is overwhelmingly important, not only for the Middle East to have some prospect of autonomy but also simply to protect U.S. interests. Though peace and regional autonomy are worthwhile goals, they are probably not attainable in the short run and are not the United States' only goals and interests. Given our ties to the region, we need a vision of the future or multiple visions that include not only an Arab-Israeli settlement but also a course if a settlement is not possible or after a settlement is reached.

Our interests at stake in the Middle East transcend Arab-Israeli matters. Although Arab-Israeli considerations have an important impact throughout the greater Middle East, they cannot dominate the affairs of the larger region. The Arabs themselves have found that other issues, which may ultimately be less important, are certainly more pressing. Iran and Iraq are pursuing their war independent of the traditional problems of the core region, and the entire eastern range of countries of the Middle East—the nations bordering on the Gulf—have not allowed their concern with the Israel and Palestine problems to prevent them from pursuing their own national and subregional interests.

The Gulf also represents a very different policy challenge to the United States than that from the other parts of the Middle East. The region is immensely important to the United States because of the West's dependence on its oil and because it holds some major mortgages on other regional policies in South and Southeast Asia, the Middle East, the Horn of Africa, and even South Africa. As we have seen, it is virtually impossible to argue against U.S. security involvement in the Gulf, given our view of our interests and the threat to them. Even if Iran were still friendly and the region stable, the United States would have difficulty taking a relaxed view of the regional powers' abilities to guarantee U.S. interests. Various possible scenarios more than meet the criteria for U.S. intervention (established earlier in this chapter), and since at least the enunciation of the Carter Doctrine in 1980, the U.S. government has committed itself to take the necessary steps to guarantee the security of the region.

Even so, some major caveats must be added to the argument for an interventionist U.S. policy in the Gulf region.

1. The United States must distinguish among the threats to its interests. Although Soviet invasion cannot be excluded, it is not the most dangerous or likely threat. Soviet-sponsored subversion, radical overthrow of Saudi Arabia and other regional regimes, decisions by incumbent governments to limit the oil flow for economic or political reasons, and domination of the region by a hostile Iran are all possible and potentially equally troublesome threats. Few of these situations would be amenable to solution by military force, especially from the United States.

2. Though much public focus has understandably been on military responses to threats in the Gulf (and that dimension is important in

signaling to the Soviets that the region is not open for poaching), military means are secondary to policy options for promoting U.S. regional interests.

3. Military means are extremely difficult and costly for the United States to bring to bear in the Gulf, and we should make every effort to reduce the chances that we will ever be called upon to back up our commitment. General nuclear war is among the more likely outcomes if we face defeat on the ground.

The advisability of the United States' playing a prominent political role in organizing Gulf security is also questionable. We carry a heavy political burden in dealing with the Gulf nations on at least two counts, and in neither case can we do much about it. A sharp reversal of our alliance with Israel is a theoretical and unattractive proposition. A rapid weaning of the advanced countries' economies from oil imports is also neither realistic nor economically desirable. A nation that has such high interests in a region tends to become part of the problem; this happened to the United States in the Gulf and in Central America. The list of threats perceived by the powers of the Gulf is similar to ours, with one or two very important exceptions. Israel is near the top of their list, the U.S. threat (intervention to keep oil flowing) occupies a high position, and the danger of direct Soviet aggression is much lower. The Gulf states rely heavily on our ultimate deterrent, they find us economically indispensable, and they are worried about many of the same threats as we are, but they (aside from the sultan of Oman) know that a close U.S. embrace would be dangerous for domestic and foreign political reasons. Nor could the United States embrace them wholeheartedly. No regime in the Gulf has high prospects for longevity (although Jordan's example shows what havoc an adroit ruler can wreak with social scientists' predictions). Although the Gulf states are not egregious human-rights violators, the gap between our values and theirs is vast, and both sides would do well to recognize the fact.

Yet, since we do share important interests, we have to reach a consensus on how to protect them. As a general principle, we can assume that the Gulf states know their problems better than we do; thus, while an on-the-ground military presence would be a more efficient way for the United States to aid them during a Soviet attack, the political damage that our presence would do to them would far outweigh the value of protection against an unlikely threat. Even second hand, our embrace can be disconcerting. One element in Pakistan's determination to maintain distance from the United States is the attitude of its Muslim brethren in the Gulf. Publicity about U.S. assistance in arming Jordanian forces for missions in the Gulf caused public-relations problems for all parties. There can be no explicit security consensus in the Southwest Asian region, only a limited but vitally important agreement on certain security contingencies. The United States must be satisified with this limitation and not seek to emphasize its involvement or demand greater and more public agreement and commitment from regional parties.

The prospects for regional cooperation among the Gulf states are good, based on a substantial tradition and shared interests. The GCC has important capabilities in countersubversion and dispute prevention, two areas in which the Gulf nations are most vulnerable. However, regional cooperation faces two difficult problems: (1) the weakness of the GCC and (2) regional deviants such as Iraq and Iran.

The United States has a modest but potentially important role to play in strengthening the GCC. In political terms, we and the Europeans could focus more attention on the council itself and support its goal of Gulf nation building. In security terms, we can provide a counter to Soviet global and regional capabilities; judicious arms sales could also play an important role. We can do much less about internal political weaknesses, although we have a strong incentive to help reduce tensions affecting the region. We must take care that our special security ties to Oman do not become a seriously divisive element within the GCC. Although our relations with Iran are virtually nonexistent, situations may arise in the future in which Iran would need support and the lower Gulf states would ask us to provide it. It would be very difficult for the United States to do anything positive about Iran, but in support of regional autonomy, we may have to swallow our pride and get on with it. It might be useful to gradually prepare U.S. public opinion for this contingency; certainly the Congress should consider the problem before it arises. Reintegration of Iran into a Gulf subsystem would not only reduce a major threat to the region but would provide a missing element of strength. The integration of Iraq as well requires a double squaring of the circle, and the Iran-Iraq war has underlined the fact that this region has one of the most intractable power balances. The first consideration for U.S. policy has had to be minimizing the danger of Soviet gains in this critical region, which means preventing the war from being subsumed into the East-West polarization. Interesting possibilities relating to the definitive ordering of power relations within the region have had to take second place. Washington has generally handled the situation skillfully and avoided overidentification with either contestant.

The United States wants to see the cold-war fault line remain as far north of the Gulf as possible, and all the regional states seem to share our view of the dangers of polarization. Our actions and especially our rhetoric should support this preference at some cost to our desire to line up support in this critical and vulnerable part of the world. Meanwhile, we must maintain the military capabilities to enable all Gulf states—including Iran—to resist Soviet encroachment, and we must ensure that our political and economic attractions continue to provide a motivation to ensure our vital access.

The Gulf presents U.S. policy with an exceptionally difficult challenge: maintaining vital interests without an assured capability to defend them. It is the prototype of this type of situation, which occurs frequently in the postimperial world. The option of controlling the Gulf unilaterally is illusory; what is left is a menu of varying degrees of cooperation with regional forces and other concerned countries that have interests parallel to our own. Since the urgency has been great, we have rapidly learned to adapt our preferences to theirs, and the results have been generally good even though the future remains uncertain. It is a lesson that we could usefully apply elsewhere.

In southern Africa, U.S. diplomacy has been generally adroit, but severe pitfalls still lie ahead. Although the 1975 involvement in Angola was a disaster precisely because it forced events into a global framework, subsequent actions of the Ford, Carter, and even the Reagan administrations have been handled largely in regional terms. In Rhodesia there was a frightening potential for an East-West overlay to the sorting out of the black-white relationship. The travails of Zimbabwe are now being worked out in domestic terms with little potential for superpower involvement. The United States also has shown sensitivity in dealing with the Namibia issue. Unfortunately, however, the presence of Cuban forces in Angola has served as a red flag for the Carter and especially the Reagan administrations. A more relaxed approach to that problem might have permitted an early settlement with Angola and improved the prospects for a settlement in Namibia. Most recently, the reported U.S. decision to provide military support for the UNITA rebel group in Angola led by Jonas Savimbi threatens a replay of the events of 1975 and an unraveling of much of the U.S. position throughout southern Africa and even beyond.

Beyond Angola and Namibia the shape of the future challenge is clear. The domestic arrangements of the Republic of South Africa promise turmoil within the country and the inevitable involvement of neighboring Black Africa, as well as much of the rest of the world. South Africa's power is so great—both internally and externally—that it may be a long while before these problems become unmanageable, even in the face of sharply increased unrest during 1985 and 1986. If the republic had embarked on even a slow and halting path toward a just society, the prospects for a largely peaceful transition would be good and would justify our tolerating a considerable amount of temporary injustice. The steps that Pretoria has taken in the early 1980s to relax petty apartheid and increase representation for Coloureds and Asians do not, however, show credible commitment toward making the basic changes needed for the black population (political representation and reversal of the homelands policy).

In handling its neighbors, Pretoria has shown even less willingness to make concessions. It has been ruthless in applying economic and military pressures on adjacent nations, none of which is strong enough to resist without extensive outside support. In the short term, the issue is the competition over the shape of the southern African subsystem. Pretoria is using its strength to create a system that it will dominate, a constellation of states that will both isolate its neighbors politically from the rest of Africa and form a *cordon sanitaire* to prevent assistance from reaching rebellious groups inside the republic. The alternative is a subsystem defined in terms of isolating South Africa as a regional deviant, based on an OAU-sponsored band of Black African states in the southern third of the continent—perhaps based on the Front Line grouping. If such a subsystem is to maintain its existence, let alone stand up to the republic, it will need a high degree of internal cohesion and substantial external support. Prospects are not bright on either count, and in terms of the criteria we have set forth for formation of state subsystems, the constellation wins easily. It would be based on power realities and would be able to exclude external (especially Soviet) intrusion.

The republic's internal arrangements and the way it runs its regional system appear to be of little concern to the United States. Solving South Africa's problems is not our responsibility; that would simply be another manifestation of intrusiveness. In any event, we lack not only the capability but also the requisite expertise and wisdom. Whites and blacks will have to work out their own salvations inside the republic, and South Africa's neighbors will have to learn to live with the process. U.S. interests in the region, and indeed in all Africa, are important but not vital. The logic of the situation is to let devolution prevail.

This arrangement, however, fails on a combination of moral and prudential counts. Apartheid is probably the worst example of large-scale deprivation of human rights in the world; we cannot remain indifferent to it any more than we can remain indifferent to communism. At issue is not just a moral principle for the mid-to-long term durability of Pretoria's domestic and regional arrangements is questionable. International opinion is so heavily against apartheid that South Africa will not be allowed to work out its own destiny. Pressures on Black African states that would join the constellation will be extreme and agonizing. It is difficult to see the current situation persisting indefinitely.

Our first concern is not to become part of the agony of southern Africa. We have no direct role to play there; the fabric of our own society probably could not bear it. Our second concern is not to stand alongside an ostracized South Africa against solid Third World opinion. We know the costs of this approach from our experiences in the Middle East. Israel may be worth the costs, but preservation of white supremacy in southern Africa is certainly not, nor are our interests in the republic (minerals, investment, sea-lane security) great enough or sufficiently threatened to warrant alignment with South Africa. Our third concern is that southern Africa not become the hunting ground of outside intruders. This is not an option that we seek; much less do we want to see the region become available to the Soviet Union, which has potential only for negative involvement. The Soviets would assert their involvement in military terms or by agitating matters and playing to the international grandstand. We are fortunate that Africans understand this concern and also realize that the United States can be helpful.

Since East-West issues are not significantly involved in southern Africa and our other interests there are not critical, we have considerable policy flexibility. We can seek out policy courses that are morally acceptable, that are useful in building systemic strength, that do not require excessive U.S. involvement, and that minimize other external involvement.

The content of U.S. policy must be clearly anti-apartheid. It should be open to discussion and modification if Pretoria makes genuine moves toward racial justice, but constructive engagement must not slip into acceptance. We should not encourage violence, both on moral grounds and because it weakens our position. If progress cannot be made through peaceful means however, we may have to adapt to violence.

We have a long task ahead in educating the U.S. public about southern African realities, and we should get on with it.

1. Since we want to keep southern Africa out of the East-West framework, we should not cast issues in those terms. Cubans and Russians have no place in the future of southern Africa unless we and our allies define them into the problem or unless the Black Africans so despair of justice that they turn to the Communist states as their last hope for assistance in a deteriorating and violent situation.

2. The United States should act as part of a larger international consensus. This vehicle of involvement has been effective in the past, it reduces our visibility and vulnerability, and it helps to keep the issue out of an East-West context. This larger consensus should continue to be based on European and like-minded states in conjunction with responsible regional states. The latter should assume as much respon-

sibility as possible, but, given South Africa's regional preponderance, they are going to need help.

3. We should not become associated with South Africa's vision of the regional subsystem as a constellation of states. It is not our responsibility to undermine it, and if Pretoria can avoid violent confrontations with Zimbabwe, Mozambique, and Angola, we should welcome it. A South African–led subsystem is not, however, viable in the long run, especially if it is designed to give legitimacy to the various South African homelands. It is thus important that there be an alternative system in place to organize and represent Balck African opinion and that it not be forced to look to the Soviet Union for support. If there is no such system, the pattern of international relations in southern Africa will be one of anarchy in the face of South African pressure, and the opportunity for meddling by outside countries will be great. The Front Line may or may not be the group to organize this system, but unless African leadership finds some alternate arrangement, the United States should give priority to helping the Front Line states strengthen their economic cooperation and withstand South African pressures.

U.S. involvement in Third World affairs has recently become most active in Central America, and this region has seen the rise of an interesting regional grouping, the Contadora Group. The Kissinger report points out that there is a direct relationship between the level of U.S. decisiveness and the momentum of Contadora.[10] Although the report may not have meant its observation in this sense, concern over U.S. intervention has grown, and the regional states have intensified their efforts to resolve regional conflict. The Contadora powers are seeking to create a framework for a settlement that would treat the United States as an outside power, whereas the United States is forcefully asserting its membership in this neighboring regional system, both through its direct role in El Salvador, Honduras, and Nicaragua and through the Caribbean Basin Initiative, which would link the entire basin more closely to the United States. What we see in Central America—not unlike in southern Africa—are competing definitions of the composition of the relevant region and debate over whether the most powerful neighboring country should act as a member of the system or as the external stimulus that promotes regional cooperation. Seen from the Central American perspective, the United States is in effect the regional deviant.

Stated another way, the issue is whether the United States accepts the fact that the process of de-imperialization is relevant and acceptable in our relations with Central America. These judgments are extremely difficult to make, and the answers are not readily evident. Our considerable strength in the region, if supported by U.S. public opinion, provides us with a wide range of policy options for the short and mid terms. At the extremes, we have the physical capability to impose our will on Central America for a considerable time, but, by the same token, our economic and other strengths guarantee that almost any outcome in Central America would ensure us abundant access to pursue our legitimate interests. A longer term prognosis is less reassuring; it would be extremely costly (hence, unpopular at home) to maintain physical domination over Central America indefinitely. This kind of protracted involvement would also probably stimulate even more anti-U.S. sentiment in the region and distaste in the international community. When we withdrew our direct presence, the regional powers would redouble their efforts to deny us access.

No U.S. policy looks to a direct, long-term military domination of Central America; the more realistic option hinges on whether the United States would be able to reshape the political and social institutions of several Central American countries relatively quickly and in ways that would enhance U.S. attractiveness to the region's peoples. This was precisely the issue posed in Vietnam. Although the two situations are very different, the Vietnam precedent highlights the kinds of difficulties that this strategy would encounter. Such an approach is more appropriate to the thinking of the Nixon Doctrine than to a strategy of devolution.

Defined somewhat differently, the U.S. approach could fall more on the side of a devolution policy, if we were to join forces with the Contadora or a similar group in facilitating the changes in El Salvador, Honduras, Guatemala, and Nicaragua that are necessary for stable regional development. For this approach to work, we and the Contadorists would have to sharply cut back our expectations. The United States would not be excluded from such a system, but its preferences also would not necessarily shape the foreign and domestic policies of even the smaller Central American nations. Although this prospect is attractive, the approach would be exceedingly hard to put into practice.

Psychological and emotional factors aside, Americans would find it difficult to accept the results of following a devolution policy—that the United States' military and security role in the region would be sharply curtailed. Although that might matter little if the regional leadership were both competent and realistic about U.S. interests in the Panama Canal and U.S.-Soviet-Cuban relationships, neither can be automatically assumed. Some element of risk would be involved, and we would not incur such risk lightly because of the proximity of Central America. Yet the U.S. military advantage is so overwhelming in the area that we could reassert our access if our vital interests were threatened and could count on public support for doing so.

An additional factor is Cuba. The Contadora powers themselves are not immune to the kinds of unrest that Cubans can fan and exploit, and they do not have proven capabilities to prevent Cuban overt or covert incursions against Guatemala, for instance. As a theoretical proposition, Cuba is more likely to "return to the hemisphere" if it can join a regional grouping that does not include the United States and that has a track record of standing up to Washington. Whether such a return could ever be more than theoretical is hard to tell; Cuban ambitions may have transcended any regional framework and may be uncontainable except by direct U.S. protection of potential targets or, indeed, by "going to the source."

A final consideration is the regional perception of the U.S. role in Central America. Arguably, we are so much a part of the problem that any movement in the region will define itself to some extent in relation to the United States. In any movements for change we are part of the target no matter what we may do. Certainly, though, lesser degrees of U.S. involvement would trigger less hostility and perhaps provide fewer opportunities for those people, such as the Cubans, whose motivations are primarily anti-American. When we define situations in Central America in terms of East-West competition, we are defining the Cubans, if not the Soviets, directly into the problem along with ourselves. Given the history of the region, this inclusion has all the makings of a prescription for disaster.

If the Kissinger Commission's observation is valid, the United States can logically best promote strong regionalism and enhance potential for devolution by increasing its levels of pressure and intervention in Central America. Even if this idea did not have a logical fallacy, it would be a very costly course by which to facilitate devolution. The logical fallacy, of course, is that beyond a certain level, U.S. strength is so great that its application would destroy the regional movement and leave behind the option of domination or anarchy. Whether by intense pressure or diplomatic maneuvering, the United States certainly has this capability in Central America.

If we would prefer to facilitate genuine devolution, our path would be more complex and would involve a measured process of disengagement. We could provide the needed resources but would have to do this in a way that did not further increase our involvement. We would need some sort of strategic screen to ensure that Cuban or even Soviet adventurism would not profit from our lesser role but only a screen that minimized the East-West overlay on regional problems. Part of the devolution process would probably involve some blustering, anti-American rhetoric and even actions. We would need to distinguish carefully (as we learned to do in dealing with Mexico) between blustering for its own sake and actions that threaten U.S. interests. It would be unrealistic to expect new forces in the region to look fondly at the U.S. historic role. Our concern is to assume a positive, nonthreatening role that can be used to define a future relationship acceptable to both sides. As always, the most useful role is for us to have strong nerves and do no harm. Although we may find it hard to accept, Central Americans must be allowed to achieve their own success and make their own mistakes, unless we are willing to bear the responsibility for these, even against their will.

In much of the Third World, implementing a policy of devolution requires little more than a change in attitude and a bit of systematic thinking on our part; existing policies have been heading in that general direction. Our range of choices is limited, and the equation, threat $\times$ interest $=$ concern, is either of such low value or so reasonably well balanced that we can afford to take some chances. Even in the Gulf we have found virtue as well as necessity in adopting a fairly low profile.

Central America is the ultimate testing site for a devolution policy. All values in the concern equation are high, and in that one region U.S. recent policies have been forcibly intrusive, if not directly interventionist. We also have some realistic options in the region for managing security unilaterally and maintaining an imperial pattern of domination. Simply because the word *imperial* is tainted is no reason to reject this course of action if it passes the test for intervention that we have set forth. I would argue that it does not, but I would concede that a case can be made as long as we are willing to carry through what we begin. Imperialism was a matter not only of capability but equally of will and self-confidence. We should ponder whether we can still sustain such requirements in a global and domestic atmosphere that has moved far in the other direction.

Whatever course of action the United States follows in Central America, it cannot serve as a model for our policy elsewhere in the Third World. If we propose to maintain the imperial order in Central America, we should recognize that each situation is unique. Elsewhere the very brief era of U.S. dominance is past; responsibility is moving back where it belongs in the hands of Third World nations themselves. Our mission is not to engage in a hopeless struggle against that change but to understand it, plan for it, and even facilitate it as we bear our global responsibilities in the postimperial order.

APPENDIX: SOME MANAGEMENT OBSERVATIONS

POLICY CONSISTENCY DEMANDS INTELLIGENT use of foreign-affairs personnel and bureaucratic machinery. Domestic consensus building is not limited to the lay public but also reaches into the bureaucracy, which generally does what elected officials want it to, provided (a) they understand what is to be done, (b) they are convinced that the administration is serious about its objectives, and (c) they sense that they have the confidence of their elected leaders. In terms of the first two points, the bureaucracy is an audience much like foreign nations, which is hardly surprisingly since it long ago learned to put itself in the shoes of others when judging the staying power of U.S. policy initiatives. Personnel of the bureaucracy will have to be part of the analytical process by which the leadership reaches its conclusions, and the new administration must come to terms with the permanent bureaucracy in a much more efficient manner than seen in our recent experiences. It is absolutely necessary that a new administration put its own people into such policymaking positions as assistant secretaryships in the Department of State and the staff of the National Security Council. The new appointees, however, must accept the fact that foreign-policy professionals at lower levels are not enemies but in virtually all instances can be enlisted to carry out the behests of their elected and appointed superiors. The bureaucracy naturally will also be the guardian of the previous writing on the foreign slate and the bearers of the bad news that certain policies cannot be implemented. They will be wrong on occasion, and new appointees should not automatically accept their arguments against policy changes; however, on balance the bureaucracy knows fairly accurately what the traffic will bear. It would be wise to come to terms with them sooner rather than later.

155

In terms of operational considerations, the U.S. government needs to better train personnel to deal with the Third World and improve the horizontal arrangements in the bureaucracy. But the quantity and quality of personnel are by and large adequate, and organizational arrangements at the working level are generally intelligent. Whatever the government's weaknesses, it does contain persons with profound knowledge of the bipolar and regional settings. Government personnel are now much better informed about the conditions, capabilities, interests, and priorities of other countries, thanks to the farseeing federal programs of the 1960s that trained a superb corps of area specialists and to the formative experiences of the two previous decades that gave rise to a remarkable sense of global awareness and responsibility. Although both of these assets are wasting, immediate problems in the bureaucracy still center on upward flow and integration of information.

An integrating mechanism is needed between the largely regional bureaucracy and the mostly generalist/globalist decisionmaking levels. This mechanism must be provided by a group that is competent, authoritative, and capable of simultaneously comprehending regional and global perspectives. The mechanism will also need a mandate for long-term planning. Short-term needs tend to be global, and the regional element usually can gain a satisfactory hearing only in terms of long-term consequences of policy choices. The bases of such groups can be found in at least two places. Although there are alternate groups that could integrate the regional, global, and functional aspects of foreign policy within the Department of State, its policy planning staff is in the best position to play the necessary role. Aside from the Department of State, the only candidate is the National Security Council (NSC) staff, which is also an integrating mechanism. The NSC staff, however, relates many other things, mainly those involving interdepartmental differences, and it has to spend much of its time on housekeeping and quasi-political duties in support of the president. The main focus would thus better remain in the Department of State. The NSC should ensure that the White House is open to the integrated advice offered by the Department of State.

Such openness is a problem all along the line, for globalist secretaries of state, as well as presidents, are not inherently receiptive to regionalist policies and advice coming up from the bureaucracy. The critical bridge within the Department of State could be established by a strong director of policy planning who has a relationship of full trust and confidence with an openminded secretary, in addition to the requisite high level of expertise on the director's staff. The conjunction of these factors within the policy planning staff has been a fairly hit-or-miss matter for years. This integrative mechanism should be strengthened still further by designating one of the most senior officials in the department to work with the planning staff as it deals with the rest of the bureaucracy and to reinforce the staff's position with the secretary. The counselor of the department is logically the most appropriate official, but the persons who have held this position have not shone very brightly in recent policy firmaments. Deputy Secretary Warren Christopher performed this function during the Carter administration, most notably in the field of human rights, but he did so less because he was given that role than because he brought quiet, consummate skill to everything he touched during those difficult four years. The existence of a high-level official charged with these responsibilities would also be extremely helpful in times of crisis when attention and involvement escalate rapidly away from the levels of bureaucracy that have detailed knowledge. This official could act as an additional channel, ensuring that intelligent and informed considerations are included in final decisions.

We must also continue to pay attention to those elements of the machine that work fairly well, since fairly well is not well enough. We should reemphasize the need to develop language skills and acquire regional knowledge. The quality of the training is not so much a problem for the government (where programs are about as good as they should be) as for the academic world. The decline in language and area studies is simply not acceptable if the United States is to continue to play a useful role in the world. Students and universities cannot be faulted for responding to the play of the market. The government has the responsibility to change the terms of the market by substantially increasing financial aid to students in needed programs and by creating employment possibilities. This approach may not appear economically rational because we would be training and employing people who for most of their productive lives would be underemployed. Yet we readily accept this situation in our armed forces, and the importance of supporting a few hundred area specialists—who will contribute to our national security—can be readily justified in comparison to supporting a few hundred thousand soldiers.

One notable danger in U.S. area programs is excessive specialization. Academic specialists on the social organization of India would be able to do a better job if they knew something about the social organization of the Sudan or Brazil, and they would have a much better conceptual grasp of their discipline. Similarly, area specialists in the government (including the foreign service) would be more effective if they had some experience in a contrasting area, and they would have a better concept of the direction of their discipline—the promotion of the U.S. national interest. A useful move that Henry Kissinger made in this direction when he was secretary of state was to require foreign service officers to have a wider diversity of assignments; these arrangements need new life breathed into them. The government might also consider providing funding for promising academic specialists to gain this kind of broadening experience—supporting, for example, a specialist on Nigerian politics for a few years in another area such as Korea or Mexico.

Possible improvement in clearance and coordination procedures within government organizations should be explored. Clearance procedures are terribly time consuming, however, and they miss the point. Checks and balances are incorporated into systems to keep them from malfunctioning, but a well-running system should not malfunction very often, and the emphasis should be on getting things right the first time. The horizons of both globalists and regionalists need to be broadened so that their development of an integrated view does not each time require a contest between opposing forces rather than a discussion of a widely shared, integrated concept.

NOTES

Chapter 1.
The Twilight of American Exceptionalism

1. Much has been written on the U.S. experience with imperialism and its painful withdrawal symptoms; the issue has occupied some of the more interesting political thinkers of our time. See, for instance, Raymond Aron, *Republique Imperiale* (Paris: Calmann-Lévy, 1973); Stanley Hoffman, *Primacy or World Order: American Foreign Policy Since the Cold War* (New York: McGraw-Hill, 1978); and George F. Kennan, *The Cloud of Danger* (Boston: Little, Brown, 1977). More specialized studies include Tony Smith, *The Pattern of Imperialism* (Cambridge: Cambridge University Press 1981); Robert A. Packenham, *Liberal America and the Third World* (Princeton, N.J.: Princeton University Press, 1973); George Liska, *Imperial America* (Baltimore: Johns Hopkins University Press, 1967); Robert W. Tucker, *Nation or Empire: The Debate over American Foreign Policy* (Baltimore: Johns Hopkins University Press, 1968); and Ronald Steel, *Pax Americana* (New York: Viking, 1967).

2. Two books illustrate this particularly well: James Thomson, Peter W. Stanley, and John C. Perry, *Sentimental Imperialists* (New York: Harper & Row, 1981), and Norman Isaacs' classic *Scratches on Our Minds,* issued in paperback as *Images of Asia* (New York: Capricorn, 1962).

3. Robert McMahon, *Colonialism and the Cold War* (Ithaca, N.Y.: Cornell University Press, 1981), p. 275, draws on U.S. archives to illustrate the dilemma posed by conflicting global and regional influences on U.S. policy toward Indonesian independence. Gary Hess, *America Encounters India, 1941–47* (Baltimore: Johns Hopkins University Press, 1971) deals with the analogous problem facing Franklin Roosevelt during World War II when U.S. support for Indian independence had to be put aside because of global demands.

4. See I. M. Destler, Leslie Gelb, and Anthony Lake, *Our Own Worst Enemy: The Unmaking of American Foreign Policy* (New York: Simon and Schuster, 1984).

Chapter 2. New Claimants for Power

1. I have described the Khrushchev approach to the Third World in Cyril Black and Thomas Perry Thornton, eds., *Communism and Revolution: The Strategic Uses of Political Violence* (Princeton, N.J.: Princeton University Press, 1964), chap. 9, and in Thornton, ed., *The Third World in Soviet Perspective* (Princeton, N.J.: Princeton University Press, 1964).

2. The post-Khrushchev shift is described in Robin Edmonds, *Soviet Foreign Policy: The Brezhnev Years* (Oxford: Oxford University Press, 1983), and Adam Ulam, *Dangerous Relations: The Soviet Union in World Politics* (New York: Oxford University Press, 1983).

3. On the growing military strength of Third World nations, see Olof Palme, ed., *Common Security—A Blueprint for Survival* (New York: Simon and Schuster, 1983); Rodney Jones and S. Hildreth, *Modern Weapons and Third World Powers* (Boulder, Colo.: Westview, 1984); Edward Kolodziej and R. Harkavy, "Developing States and the International Security System," *Journal of International Affairs* 34, no. 1 (spring/summer 1980), pp. 59ff.; and J. S. Mehta, ed., *Third World Militarization* (Austin, Tex.: Lyndon B. Johnson School of Public Affairs, 1985).

4. Hedley Bull provides a useful summary of the factors restraining external intervention in the Third World in *Intervention in World Politics* (Oxford: Clarendon Press, 1984), chap. 9.

Chapter 3. Global and Regional Systems

1. The theoretical literature on regionalism, often coupled with symposiums covering various regions of the world, has flourished in the last decade or so. Among the most helpful works are Gavin Boyd, ed., *Regionalism and Global Security* (Lexington, Mass.: Lexington Books, 1984), especially Boyd's opening and closing chapters; Lewis Cantori and S. Spiegel, *The International Politics of Regions* (Englewood Cliffs, N.J.: Prentice-Hall, 1970); Werner Feld and G. Boyd, *Comparative Regional Systems* (New York: Pergamon, 1980); Richard Falk and S. Mendlovitz, *Regional Politics and World Order* (San Franciso: W. H. Freeman, 1973); Robert Keohane and J. Nye, *Power and Independence* (Boston: Little, Brown, 1977); James Rosenau, Kenneth W. Thomspon, and Gavin Boyd, *World Politics—An Introduction* (New York: Free Press, 1976); Joseph Nye, *Peace in Parts* (Boston: Little, Brown, 1971); Bruce Russet, *The International Regions and the International System* (Westwood, Conn.: Greenwood, 1975); and, George Liska's most stimulating *States in Evolution* (Baltimore: Johns Hopkins University Press, 1973), as well as his "The Third World: Regional Systems and Global Order," in *Retreat from Empire?* ed. Robert Osgood et al. (Baltimore: Johns Hopkins University Press, 1973). Worthwhile shorter pieces include John Stremlau, "The Foreign Policies of the Developing Countries in the 1980s," *Journal of International Affairs* 34, no. 1 (spring/summer 1981), pp. 161ff.; W. R. Thompson, "The Regional Subsystem: A Conceptual Explication and Propositional Inventory," *International Studies Quarterly* 17, no. 1 (March 1973), pp. 89ff.; A. P. Rana, "Regionalism as an Approach to International

Order: A Conceptual Overview," *International Studies* (Delhi) 18, no. 4 (October/December 1979); and, Barry Buzan, "Regional Security as a Policy Objective," in *The Great Game*, ed. A. Z. Rubinstein (New York: Praeger, 1983), pp. 238ff.

2. An instructive parallel in systemic relationships, relating the "little" traditions of Indian villages to the "great" Indian classical tradition, is set forth in McKim Marriott, *Village India* (Chicago: University of Chicago Press, 1955), pp. 176–78.

3. See especially Liska, *States in Evolution*, on this key point.

4. I. William Zartman, in Falk and Mendlovitz, *Regional Politics and World Order*, p. 387.

5. I am indebted to Evelyn Colbert for the parallel.

6. Additional information on the regional influentials can be found in Jones and Hildreth, *Modern Weapons and Third World Powers*, chap. 2, and by Wolf Grabendorff, "The Role of Regional Powers in the Central American Crisis," in *Latin American Foreign Policies—A Comparative Approach*, ed. H. Muñoz and J. Tulchin (Boulder, Colo.: Westview, 1983).

Chapter 4. Relating to the Third World

1. Jones and Hildreth, in *Modern Weapons and Third World Powers*, pp. 85–88, provide a discussion of the access problem. The Overseas Development Council (ODC) has been extremely active in educating Americans about their responsibilities in the Third World. See their annual *Agendas* and especially John Sewell and J. Mathieson, *The Ties that Bind: U.S. Interests in the Third World* (Washington: ODC, 1982). An excellent overall view is provided by Richard E. Feinberg, *The Intemperate Zone: The Third World Challenge to U.S. Foreign Policy* (New York: Norton, 1983). Feinberg's exploration of the issues is from a primarily economic perspective, but it is broadly parallel to mine.

2. The costs, however, are high and place distinct limits on what the Soviets can hope to achieve in the Third World. See Charles Wolf, *The Costs of Soviet Empire* (Santa Monica, Calif.: Rand Corporation, 1983).

3. This concept is emphasized by John Girling, *America and the Third World* (London: Routledge and Kegan-Paul, 1980). The economic motivation is argued by Joyce and Gabriel Kolko, *The Limits of Power: The World and U.S. Foreign Policy, 1945–54* (New York: Harper & Row, 1972).

4. For a similar discussion of the conditions of U.S. intervention, specifically in Latin America, see Cole Blasier, *The Giant's Rival* (Pittsburgh: University of Pittsburgh Press, 1983), chap. 7.

5. Cited in Richard Kirkendall, *A Global Power—America Since the Age of Roosevelt*, 2nd ed. (New York: Knopf, 1980), p. 202.

6. In addition to Girling, *America and the Third World*, see Mel Gurtov, *The United States Against the Third World* (New York: Praeger, 1974); Richard Barnet, *Intervention and Revolution* (New York: World Publishing, 1968); and the symposium, William Taubman, ed., *Globalism and its Critics* (Lexington, Mass.: Heath, 1973). The tone of much of this material is shrill, and it is

occasionally badly marred by the difficult intellectual climate of the post-Vietnam years; nevertheless, several of these studies are stimulating, in the material that they present and in the framework in which they place it. A conservative response in kind is W. Scott Thompson, ed., *The Third World—Premises of U.S. Policy* (San Francisco: Institute for Contemporary Studies, 1978).

7. Henry A. Kissinger, *The White House Years* (Boston: Little, Brown, 1979), pp. 888ff.

8. Lloyd and Susanne Rudolph offer a sophisticated and well-documented proregionalist argument in "The Coordination of Complexity in South Asia," the opening chapter of the 1975 study prepared for the Commission on the Organization of the Government for the Conduct of Foreign Policy (the Murphy Commission). It has been republished as *The Regional Imperative* (Atlantic Highlands, N.J.: Humanities Press, 1980).

9. Problems of pursuing new issues are illustrated in the example of Pakistan in my "Between the Stools? U.S. Policy Toward Pakistan During the Carter Administration," *Asian Studies* 22, no. 10 (October 1982), pp. 959ff.

Chapter 5. The Choice of Strategies

1. Robert Keohane, in much the same terms, makes the case for the decline in U.S. economic hegemony but also notes the need for continued leadership from Washington in his *After Hegemony: Cooperation and Discord in the World Political Economy* (Princeton, N.J.: Princeton University Press, 1984).

2. The title of an article in A. Z. Rubinstein, ed., *Soviet and Chinese Influence in the Third World* (New York: Praeger, 1975). Rubinstein is also editing a series of studies illustrating the problems of defining, acquiring, and maintaining influence in Third World relationships with major power patrons. See, for instance, Robert Horn, *Soviet-Indian Relations: Issues and Influence* (New York: Praeger, 1982).

3. Henry A. Kissinger, *Years of Upheaval* (Boston: Little, Brown, 1982), chaps. 11–12, especially p. 579. For a critical assessment of the 1972 agreement and its results, see Alexander L. George, ed., *Managing US-Soviet Rivalry: Problems of Crisis Prevention* (Boulder, Colo.: Westview, 1983), especially chaps. 5 and 7.

4. Zbigniew Brzezinski, *Power and Principle* (New York: Farrar-Strauss, 1983), p. 148.

5. Cited by C. W. Maynes, in "Old Errors in the New Cold War," *Foreign Policy*, no. 46 (spring 1982), p. 102.

6. Brzezinski, *Power and Principle,* pp. 53–55.

7. See Stanley Hoffman, "Requiem," *Foreign Policy,* no. 42, (spring 1981), pp. 2ff., for an elegant statement in the shift in Carter's foreign-policy emphasis. Carter's memoirs, *Keeping Faith* (New York: Bantam Books, 1982), which were written after he left office, hardly mention the Third World and North-South matters except to the extent that Third World countries were involved in the major crises of his adminstration.

Chapter 6. The Situation in Individual Regions

1. Several of the symposiums listed in note 1 of Chapter 3 contain useful coverage of individual regions by area specialists. A selection of other material can be found under the individual section headings of Chapter 6.

2. An extensive literature has been written on Southeast Asia—on both the ASEAN grouping and its relations with Vietnam, China, and the superpowers. The following books and articles were particularly helpful to me: Robert Scalapino and Yusuf Wanandi, eds., *Economic, Political and Security Issues in Southeast Asia in the 1980s* (Berkeley: University of California Press, 1982); William Tow and W. Feeney, *U.S. Foreign Policy and Asian-Pacific Security: A Transregional Approach* (Boulder, Colo.: Westview, 1982); Michael Leifer, *Conflict and Regional Order in Southeast Asia* (London: International Institute for Strategic Studies, Adelphi Paper no. 162, 1980); Sheldon Simon, *The ASEAN States and Regional Security* (Palo Alto, Calif.: Hoover Institution, 1982); Lucian Pye, *Redefining American Policy in Southeast Asia* (Washington: American Enterprise Institute, 1982); Arnfinn Jorgensen-Dahl, *Regional Organization and Order in South-east Asia* (New York: St. Martin's, 1982); Les Buszynski, "The Soviet Union and Southeast Asia after the Fall of Saigon," *Asian Survey* 21, no. 5 (May 1981), pp. 536ff.; Bernard Gordon, "Asian Angst and American Foreign Policy," *Foreign Policy,* no. 47 (summer 1982), pp. 46ff.; Thomas Wilborn, "The Soviet Union and ASEAN," in *The Soviet Union in the Third World: Successes and Failures,* ed. Robert Donaldson (Boulder, Colo.: Westview, 1981); Franklin Weinstein, "The U.S. Role in East and Southeast Asia," in *A U.S. Foreign Policy for Asia,* ed. Ramon Myers (Palo Alto, Calif.: Hoover Institution, 1982); and, Richard Solomon, "Coalition Building or Condominium?" in *Soviet Policy in East Asia,* ed. Donald Zagoria (New Haven, Conn.: Yale University Press, 1982).

3. William Barnds's *India, Pakistan and the Great Powers* (New York: Praeger, 1972) remains the best comprehensive view of the subject. More recent events are covered by Surjit Mansingh, *India's Search for Power* (New Delhi: Sage Publications, 1984), especially chaps. 5 and 6. More specific pieces on South Asia as a region include my "South Asia and the Great Powers," *World Affairs* 132, no. 4 (March 1970), pp. 345ff.; P. M. Mishra, "Determinants of Intra-regional Relations in South Asia," *India Quarterly,* 36, no. 6 (January-March 1980), pp. 68ff.; the chapters by Leo Rose in Feld and Boyd, *Comparative Regional Systems,* and by Walter Andersen in Myers, *A U.S. Foreign Policy for Asia.* See also Lloyd and Susanne Rudolph, *The Regional Imperative,* as well as their chapter, "The United States and South Asia," in *U.S. Foreign Policy and the Third World: Agenda 1983,* ed. John Lewis (New York: Praeger, 1983). Zalmay Khalilzad, Timothy George, Robert Litwak, and Shahram Chubin, *Security in Southern Asia* (New York: St. Martin's, 1984), examine South Asian regionalism and U.S. policy in chaps. 11 and 12 (by Shahram Chubin).

4. Kissinger, *The White House Years,* chap. 21. For a rebuttal, see Christopher Van Hollen, "The Tilt Policy Revisted: Nixon-Kissinger Geopolitics in South Asia," *Asian Survey* 20, no. 4 (April 1980), pp. 339ff.

5. This is discussed in Thornton, "Between the Stools?" and "American Interest in India Under Carter and Reagan," *SAIS Review* 5, no. 1 (winter/ spring 1985).

6. On the Soviet invasion of Afghanistan, see Bhabani Sen Gupta, *The Afghan Syndrome* (London: Croom Helm, 1982); Thomas Hammond, *Red Flag over Afghanistan* (Boulder, Colo.: Westview, 1983); and, Henry Bradsher, *Afghanistan and the Soviet Union* (Durham, N.C.: Duke University Press, 1983).

7. The beginnings of SARC are discussed in Dieter Braun's *Südasien zwischen Konflikten und Zusammenarbeit* (Ebenhausen: Stiftung Wissenschaft und Politik, 1983). The April 1985 issue of *Asian Studies* (25, no. 4) contains a series of articles examining SARC from various points of view.

8. For a discussion of the problem that the United States encounters in dealing with South Asia as a discrete region (rather than as an adjunct of Southeast or Southwest Asia) see Thomas P. Thornton, "U.S.-Indian Relations and South Asian Security Issues," in Robert Scalapino and Nur Hussain, eds., *United States-Pakistan Relations* (Berkeley, Calif.: University of California Press, 1986).

9. The literature on the Middle East is vast. Fortunately, L. Carl Brown's *International Politics and the Middle East: Old Rules, Dangerous Game* (Princeton, N.J.: Princeton University Press, 1984) offers an excellent perspective on Middle East problems that is particularly relevant for the approach I have taken in this book. Brown includes an excellent bibliographic essay to which the interested reader is referred. I would single out only a few items. Two pioneering studies of the Middle East in systemic terms deserve mention: Leonard Binder, "The Middle East as a Subordinate International System," *World Politics* 10, no. 3 (April 1958), pp. 408ff., and Michael Brecher, "The Middle East Subordinate State System and its Impact on Israel's Foreign Policy," *International Studies Quarterly* 12, no. 2 (June 1969), pp. 117ff. I also found helpful two books that came out after Brown's; Robert O. Freedman, ed., *The Middle East Since Camp David* (Boulder, Colo.: Westview, 1984), and Bahgat Korany and Ali E. Hillal Dessouki, eds., *The Foreign Policies of the Arab States* (Boulder, Colo.: Westview, 1984), especially the chapter by Paul C. Noble, "The Arab System: Opportunities, Constraints and Pressures."

On the Gulf, see the chapters by Gary Sick and Michael Sterner in A. Z. Rubinstein, ed., *The Great Game: Rivalry in the Persian Gulf and South Asia* (New York: Praeger, 1983); James Noyes, *The Clouded Lens* (Palo Alto, Calif.: Hoover Institution, 1979); Shahram Chubin, *The Role of Outside Powers* (Totowa, N.J.: Allanheld, Osmun, 1981); Anthony H. Cordesman, *The Gulf and the Search For Strategic Stability* (Boulder, Colo.: Westview, 1984); Thomas McNaugher, "Balancing Soviet Power in the Persian Gulf," *Brookings Review* (summer 1983), pp. 20ff.; Christopher Van Hollen, "Don't Engulf the Gulf," *Foreign Affairs* 59, no. 5 (summer 1981), pp. 1064ff.; David Newsom, "America Engulfed," *Foreign Policy*, no. 43 (summer 1981), pp. 33ff. On the GCC, see Ursula Braun, *Der Golf-Kooperationsrat: Profil, Potential, Verflechtungen* (Ebenhausen: Stiftung Wissenschaft und Politik, SWP-S 320, Fo.Pl. IV.3c/85, October 1985).

10. For Brecher's and Binder's models of the Middle East system (concentric circles versus separate subregions), see the two articles cited in the previous note.

11. Brown, *International Politics and the Middle East,* pp. 16, 190ff.

12. The word *cento* is Latin in origin and means "a garment of patchwork." The *Oxford English Dictionary* gives some delightful usage examples, including the musing of a seventeenth-century missionary: "There is under these centoes and miserable outsides . . . a soul of the same alloy with our owne."

13. A general survey is offered by Jennifer Whitaker, ed., *Africa and the United States* (New York: New York University Press, 1979); especially useful is Henry Bienen's contribution to Lewis, ed., *U.S. Foreign Policy and the Third World: Agenda 1983),* as well as his "Perspectives on Soviet Intervention in Africa," *Political Science Quarterly* 95, no. 1 (spring 1980), pp. 29ff. There is good material in Alfred Hero and J. Barratt, eds., *The American People and South Africa: Publics, Elites and Policymaking* (Lexington, Mass.: Lexington Books, 1981), notably the contribution by Chester Crocker. *Orbis* 25, no. 4 (winter 1982) contains a number of interesting pieces on Africa, including W. Scott Thompson's "U.S. Policy Towards Africa: At America's Service?"

14. Nigeria's position is discussed by Timothy Shaw, "Nigeria in the International System," in *The Political Economy of Nigeria,* ed. I. William Zartman (New York: Praeger, 1983).

15. Among the extensive works on southern African issues, those especially important for my concerns were two Adelphi Papers issued by the London International Institute for Strategic Studies: Garrick Uttley's *Globalism or Regionalism? U.S. Policy Towards Southern Africa,* no. 154 (1979), and Robert Jaster's exemplary *A Regional Security Role for Africa's Front-Line States,* no. 180 (1983). See also "South Africa: Strategy for Change," by Chester Crocker, in *Foreign Affairs* 59, no. 2 (winter 1980/81), which set the basic framework for the Reagan administration's policy in the region. For recent analyses that focus on South Africa's attempts to dominate its neighbors and on the regional responses, see Gerald J. Bender, James S. Coleman, and Richard L. Sklar, eds., *African Crisis Areas and U.S. Foreign Policy* (Berkeley: University of California Press, 1985), especially chapter 3 by Robert Price; and Robert I. Rotberg, Henry S. Bienen, Robert Legvold, and Gavin G. Maasdorp, *South Africa and Its Neighbors: Regional Security and Self Interest* (Lexington, Mass.: Lexington Books, 1985).

16. On Angola, see John Marcum, "Lessons of Angola," *Foreign Affairs* 54, no. 3 (April 1976), pp. 407ff., and Gerald Bender, "Kissinger in Angola: Anatomy of a Failure," in *American Policy in Southern Africa,* ed. Rene Lemarchand (Washington: University Press of America, 1978), pp. 63ff.

17. Paul Henze provides an informed discussion of U.S. policy in the Horn of Africa in Walter Laqueur, ed., *The Pattern of Soviet Conduct in the Third World* (New York: Praeger, 1983).

18. On the Latin American system in general, see G. Pope Atkins, *Latin America in the International Political System* (New York: Free Press, 1977); Tom J. Farer, ed., *The Future of the Inter-American System* (New York: Praeger,

1979); Gordon Connell-Smith, *The U.S. and Latin America: An Historical Analysis of Inter-American Relations* (New York: Wiley, 1974); and, Arthur P. Whitaker, *The Western Hemisphere Idea: Its Rise and Decline* (Ithaca, New York: Cornell University Press, 1954). Several recent works dealing specifically with Central America are Bruce Michael Bagley, *Regional Powers and the Caribbean Basin* (Washington, D.C.: Johns Hopkins School of Advanced International Studies, Central American and Caribbean Program, Occasional Paper no. 2, 1983); Richard Fagen and Olga Pellicer, eds., *The Future of Central American Policy: Choices for the United States and Mexico* (Palo Alto, Calif.: Stanford University Press, 1983); Wolf Grabendorff, "The Role of Regional Powers in the Central American Crisis," in *Latin American Foreign Policies— A Comparative Approach,* ed. Muñoz and Tulchin; Abraham Lowenthal and S. Wells, eds., *The Central American Crisis: Policy Perspectives* (Washington, D.C.: The Wilson Center, Latin American Program, Working Paper no. 119, 1982); Wolf Grabendorff et al., eds., *Political Change in Central America: Internal and External Dimensions* (Boulder, Colo.: Westview, 1984); and Susan Kaufman Purcell, "Demystifying Contadora," *Foreign Affairs* 64, no. 1 (fall 1985), pp. 74–95.

19. See Richard Feinberg, "The Recent Radical Redefinition of U.S. Interests and Diplomacy in Central America," in *Central America: International Dimensions of the Crisis,* ed. Richard Feinberg (New York: Holmes and Meier, 1982). The parallel to the policy shifts I have described in the case of South Asia (see chap. 5, note 9) is striking.

Chapter 7. Policy Directions

1. In the words of Alexander Haig (who was certainly in a position to know): "Of the many destructive effects of Vietnam and Watergate, none is worse than the tendency of a new administration to believe that history began on its Inauguration Day, and its predecessor was totally wrong about everything, and that all of its acts must therefore be cancelled. This produces a policy of recrimination rather than a policy of renewal; it causes men and women to look back in anger rather than to look forward in hope and confidence." (*Time,* 2 April 1984, 50).

2. A similar mixed pattern would emerge if we had discussed all the other Third World regions, but among them, only Northeast Asia would come anywhere near the Persian Gulf in terms of serious interests under threat

3. Specific proposals of a managerial nature are in the appendix. I have offered some suggestions about dealing with the Soviet Union in Chapter 2.

4. See Feinberg, *The Intemperate Zone;* also Robert Rothstein, *The Third World and U.S. Foreign Policy* (Boulder, Colo.: Westview, 1981), which addresses economic aspects of U.S.–Third World relations.

5. Ankie Hoogvelt rejects the idea that reformist policies would be able to do anything for Third World problems. Although I do not share her deterministic pessimism, I agree with her surprisingly, un-Marxist concern for "saving one's own soul" by supporting measures aimed at ameliorating the lot of Third World

peoples. In her *The Third World and Global Development* (London: Macmillan, 1982), p. 212, she concluded: "I believe that we must fight, not in order to win (I do not think that we can) but in order to retain our human dignity." That should be rationale enough for Marxist and non-Marxist alike.

6. "Implications of a Foreign Policy of Restraint," *Foreign Service Journal* 47, no. 11 (November 1970), p. 39.

7. These criteria seem compatible with the ones set forth by Secretary of Defense Caspar Weinberger (*New York Times,* November 29, 1984). It is noteworthy that such a restrictive approach was outlined by the head of the military department—which would bear the responsibilty of carrying out any military intervention.

8. Sheldon Simon raises the interesting possibility of a multilateralization of the Philippine bases under which ASEAN forces would use some of them as a means of demonstrating that the bases serve not only U.S. interests ("The Great Powers and Southeast Asia," *Asian Survey* 25, no. 9, September 1985), p. 930.

9. "Assad and the Future of the Middle East," *Foreign Affairs* 62, no. 2 (winter 1983/84), p. 246.

10. *Report of the National Bipartisan Commission on Central America* (Washington, D.C.: Government Printing Office, 1984), p. 120.

INDEX